Praise for BEING THE PRESENCE OF CHRIST

This book is food for all who are hungry for an inner transformation in their lives. Tapping into the ancient spiritual practices, Daniel Vestal connects biblically based mysticism with evangelism and social justice.

—TONY CAMPOLO
Eastern University

The most precious gifts often come in deceptively small packages. *Being the Presence of Christ* is such a precious gift. Drawing on a lifetime of visionary church leadership, Daniel Vestal provides us with this simple yet profoundly wise guide to being the presence of Christ to one another. Vestal's powerful little book cuts to the heart of the Christian good news and challenges us and then shows us the way to embody—not just believe—the teachings of Jesus.

—DIANA GARLAND, PhD
Dean, Baylor University
School of Social Work

In this much needed and easy-to-read primer on the good news of the Christian gospel, Daniel Vestal extends a warm invitation to experience—as he has—the transforming presence of Christ. "As we are redeemed and transformed, we become better able to be the life-changing presence of Christ in our world." Truly good news!

—MARGARET CAMPBELL
Chair, Renovaré Ministry Team

Daniel Vestal's book is one of the most accessible and winsome introductions to the spiritual formation paradigm for Christian living and for leading the church that I've read in quite a while. Daniel's vision of Christian spirituality and the path of transformation is authentic and sound, and he presents it in a personal way that will bless anyone seeking a deeper life with God.

What makes this book uniquely valuable, however, is Daniel's grasp of Christian spiritual formation combined with his great knowledge of congregational life and pastoral leadership. He sets the agenda for a new vision and way of being church and leading church: guiding people to receive and to practice and to be the presence of Christ in the world.

—STEPHEN BRYANT
World Editor and Publisher
The Upper Room

Each section of this book adds another element to the challenge of living as a Christian in the world. Daniel Vestal offers a comprehensive view on the being and doing of faith. Having worked with the author for several years, I see his life and work in the principles on these pages. This book has integrity because Daniel Vestal has struggled with the challenges he lays before us.

—DAVID L. ODOM
Executive Director
Leadership Education at Duke Divinity School

Being the Presence of Christ

A Vision for Transformation

Daniel Vestal

UPPER
ROOM BOOKS®
NASHVILLE

Cover design: Bruce Gore / www.gorestudio.com
Cover image: Getty Images
Interior design: PerfecType, Nashville, TN
First printing: 2008

LIBRARY OF CONGRESS CATALOGING-IN-PUBLICATION DATA
Vestal, Daniel
  Being the presence of Christ : a vision for transformation / Daniel Vestal.
    p. cm.
  ISBN 978-0-8358-9965-9
  1. Jesus Christ—Presence. I. Title.
  BT590.P75V47 2008
  248.4—dc22   2008015798

Printed in the United States of America

CONTENTS

ACKNOWLEDGMENTS

This book is dedicated to two Christian scholars who have mentored me through their writings: William P. Clemmons, a contemplative, and Alan Neely, a missiologist. I am grateful for their influence on my life.

I am especially thankful for the editors at Upper Room Books, Robin Pippin and Jeannie Crawford-Lee, who have offered encouragement and valuable counsel. Also Carla Wynn Davis provided helpful suggestions about the manuscript. My administrative assistant, Charlotte Taylor, is a colleague and friend without whom this project could not have been completed.

INTRODUCTION

As human beings, we can be dwellings for the living Christ. We can be a continuous embodiment and incarnation of Jesus Christ in the world.

We can be the presence of Christ to one another and the world. It's a simple yet profound truth that could revolutionize our lives and our world. It's the concept that each of us can be a sanctuary where Jesus Christ lives. Our spirits can be in communion with the eternal Spirit. Our bodies can be a temple of the Holy. Our daily existence can reflect and radiate the beauty and truth of the Incarnate Son of God.

To be and act as Christ's presence is the clarifying and unifying vision I wish to set forth in this book. It is a vision that has captured me and consumes me. The sheer wonder of being Christ's presence humbles and overwhelms me. At times I can hardly believe it is possible. At other times I can hardly believe anything else matters. This is not a new vision, of course, but one shared by the very first followers of Christ.

Those first Christians lived in a world dominated by idolatry, totalitarian rule, and the practice of magical arts. Greek philosophy and Roman paganism shaped the cultural context, as did belief in demons and the supernatural. It was a time of political unrest and social ferment. The world order and the established Jewish religion were hostile to the Christians' new way. Christians were few in numbers, and even fewer could be called rich or powerful.

Yet in such an environment Christians boldly proclaimed that Jesus Christ had been raised from the dead, was reigning as the Lord of all, and would return soon. They believed that his living presence was real by the gift of the Holy Spirit and that they somehow were a part of what God was doing in the world because Christ was among them and within them.

Today we live in a very different world from that of the first Christians. Ours is a global village bound together by technology and rapid communication. A belief in demons has been replaced by psychology and belief in human capability. Greek philosophy has given way to other world views: scientism, secularism, relativism. Roman paganism is not popular but different kinds of paganism are, such as the unbridled pursuit of sexual gratification and the quest for material possessions.

Political unrest and social ferment persist. Some consider the past century the most violent in human history. Our global village is deeply divided by walls of religion, race and politics. And with all of our technological and economic advances, there is an inexcusable divide between rich and poor as well as an environmental threat to human existence on our planet.

Yet, we live in a world of increased and intensified interest in spirituality, the mysterious, the transcendent, the supernatural, and the paranormal. More and more people watch television shows and movies with spiritual themes. More and more books deal with religion, the occult, New Age topics, metaphysics, and inspiration. For all our fascination with entertainment and money, we still search for meaning in life; and the deepest yearnings of the human spirit are unsatisfied. The explosion of technology has given us instant access to greater amounts of information. It has made opportunities once reserved for a few available to many. But the availability of information does not guarantee moral clarity, personal fulfillment, or spiritual illumination. It doesn't necessarily create community, passion for justice, or capacity for sacrifice.

The Christian Gospel

Even in a world like ours, the Christian gospel is still powerful, changing more lives than we can know. It still offers a profound intellectual and philosophical framework for life, a compelling worldview, and a coherent ethic for moral decision making. But even beyond all this is a profound experience both personal and communal. The Christian experience encompasses the total human personality and the total human family. It is an experience evidenced by joy, peace, and love grounded in the resurrection of Jesus Christ.

The Christian gospel boldly celebrates and proclaims that Jesus Christ is alive. He lives not just as a memory among those who follow his teachings, but he himself lives. The very one who walked on this earth as a prophet, teacher, and miracle-worker was raised from the dead after his cruel crucifixion. The Christian gospel proclaims and celebrates that, but it doesn't end there. On the day of Pentecost, a Spirit was given to live among and within all who confess Jesus as Lord, and that Spirit is none other than the Spirit of Jesus Christ. So the Christian gospel further affirms the amazing fact that Jesus is not limited to one time and one place as he was during his earthly ministry. Now as the risen, reigning Lord of the cosmos, Jesus lives by his spirit in all who believe in him, love him, and follow him. Christ lives in us.

As human beings, we can be dwellings for the living Christ. We can be a continuous embodiment and incarnation of Jesus Christ in the world. As individuals and as members of a community, we can be the presence of Christ. For me, this is what it means to be a Christian. But it is also, for me, what it takes to transform ourselves, our society, and our world.

In this book I want to set forth an incredibly wonderful message that is both challenging and hopeful. The challenge in becoming the presence of Christ is that many of our prejudices and patterns of living need to be altered. The hope is knowing such transformation is possible. The challenge is that our segregated, gentrified, hostile, and at times violent society is declared unacceptable to the God who created us and loves us. But the hope is that it is possible for all this to change. Not suddenly and surely not without great upheaval, but by the presence and power of Jesus Christ working in and through us, all this can change.

Being the presence of Christ is the way of transformation—physical, spiritual, individual, social, and cosmic. As human beings, we cannot be divided up neatly into categories. We cannot be transformed by just changing parts of our life. We are too mysteriously and beautifully woven together for transformation to occur only in part.

Transforming the whole is what matters. That transformation makes the presence of Christ powerful not only to individuals but to the entire human community. We are woven together as a human family, which means that my personal transformation is tied to the transformation of others. I can never be fully whole until all are whole. Sometimes transformation happens from the inside out, that is, the individual influences the community. And sometimes it happens from outside in, that is, the community acts on the individual. But in either case, the goal is always the same—transformation of the human character and human culture.

Deep within us we yearn to be a part of the transformation of the world and to participate in our own transformation. Yet most of us will not discover the AIDS vaccine, have millions to give to charity, or be a celebrity. We will live our lives within limited confines of family, friends, and community; but we long and yearn and sometimes even ache for a new world order. That yearning may ebb and flow but lives within us. Being the presence of Christ fulfills that yearning and is the means by which it can be fulfilled.

Scope and Structure

This book is written by a Christian for Christians. At the same time, I intend it to be an apologetic and an appeal for non-Christians. It is an effort to interpret the Christian gospel in ways that can be appreciated and understood by both people in the church and those outside the church. I hope people of other faiths and people of goodwill might consider how the Christian vision speaks to them.

I realize that I often use language and Bible references in ways that may be confusing to some. I'm not trying to hide my reasoning behind a "code language" of theology. But it is simply impossible for me to present the meaning of the Christian gospel without using language and references that the gospel itself creates.

This book can be read from beginning to end, from the end to the beginning, or from the middle in either direction. Its message resembles a circle with several entry points more than a straight line from one point to the next. With this in mind, let me offer a brief preview of each chapter.

- Chapter 1 is about beginnings. The Christian gospel begins with the resurrection of Jesus Christ from the dead. All the documents that Christians call the New Testament were written from the perspective of the risen Christ. They each bear the stamp of conviction that Jesus has risen from the dead and lives by his Spirit in all who receive him.

- Chapter 2 considers the basics. What is absolutely essential to the lifelong experience of being the presence of Christ? What is central to this vision and core to this way of living?

- Chapters 3 and 4 discuss prayer. God is always present to us and always pursuing us, blessing us, and loving us. Prayer is then living in response to God's presence and engaging in actions that keep us responsive and attentive. It is literally "practicing the presence of Christ."

- Chapter 5 concerns personal transformation. The root of the world's problems lies in the human heart, which means that the most needed changes are internal and spiritual. The presence of Christ transforms us as persons.

- Chapter 6 examines Christian community. All who experience the presence of Christ are inextricably bound together. We are Christ's body and must learn how to live out this reality with others.

- Chapter 7 explores the mystery of human suffering. The defining symbol of Christianity is the cross, and we are invited not only to believe in the cross for our own salvation but to embrace it as a way of life.

- Chapter 8 explains Christlikeness through service, especially as it has to do with practical involvement with people. To be the presence of Christ means we will be servant to others, ministering to their needs and helping them in the same way Christ did.

- Chapter 9 investigates a Christian social ethic. The transformation of society is one of the goals of the Christian vision. We cannot ignore the great injustices and inequities in the world by living privately, comfortably, and selfishly.

If you would like a study guide to accompany your own reading or to use in a small group, there is one available online. You may access it at www.thefellowship.info/beingthepresenceofchrist.

I write this book as one who has lived most of my life as Christian. Though I have had my intellectual struggles and personal disappointments, I have never left the Christian faith. My understanding of others' doubts, dilemmas, and despair regarding the Christian faith is limited. However, my experience has created an opportunity to explore the Christian faith from the inside and ask the question, "What is the really good news that the Christian Gospel claims to possess and proclaim?" Of course, there are many answers to that question, but I seek to offer my own in this book. It has come out of a life enriched by many mentors and teachers. I have seen this faith lived out in simple souls, in sophisticated scholars, and in ardent activists. I have observed individuals whose profound expressions of Christian faith have been forged in suffering and struggle. I owe so much to so many who have been the presence of Christ to me and before me, and now I seek to offer my voice as a witness to this Gospel as I understand it.

CHAPTER 1

Beginnings
Receiving
the Presence of Christ

Receiving the presence of Christ is receiving Christ himself—the selfsame one who lived, died, and rose again. But now his presence is invisible to our natural eyes because these eyes can see only what is finite. Christ is now infinite, unlimited, eternal, and cosmic. Such reality cannot be contained, controlled, or confined. But such reality can be received.

First Steps

How do we receive Christ's presence today? We choose it. We respond to our life experiences, and we ask for Christ's presence in our lives. Christ never coerces us but waits for our consent. When we give it, no matter how tentative or faulty, he communicates and communes with us in very personal yet profound ways. Christ comes to us with love, acceptance, grace, and goodness.

An epiphany or experience of the presence, power, and reality of Jesus Christ surpasses an emotional or intellectual experience, although emotions and intellect may be involved. The experience lies outside the bounds of sensory perception, although the senses may be involved. It is spiritual and it is mystery. To receive the presence of Christ is more akin to being known than to knowing, to being apprehended than apprehending. This is the experience of pure gift. It cannot be forced or faked—only "faithed."

Receiving the presence of Christ is like illumination or inspiration. However frail or fallen we may be, if we desire the presence of Christ, we need only say yes, and it comes. Christ comes.

> Like fire
> Like water
> Like light
> Like morning after the dark night
> Like a friend you've always known but never known
> Like a lover that has found a beloved
> Like a parent welcoming a wayward child
> Like a mother embracing a baby

Christ comes in surprising ways—amazing ways. John Wesley described his heart being "strangely warmed." Blaise Pascal, French mathematician and philosopher, referred to his dramatic spiritual experience with the words, "Fire, the God of Abraham, the God of Isaac, the God of Jacob, not the God of the philosophers and scribes. Certainty, certainty and emotion, joy, peace, God of Jesus Christ."

Mystics and martyrs, philosophers and poets, young and old, rich and poor, educated and uneducated have given common testimony to the experience of receiving Christ. Some have had dreams and visions, and others have laughed and wept—at the same time. Some have trembled or shaken, while still others have sat absolutely still with nothing but quiet confidence.

Receiving Christ may be accompanied by amazing phenomena or it may not. What is important is the consent, the voluntary act of acquiescence. As we open our mind and heart, the unseen One comes to us in our spirit, not only to awaken and quicken us but to win our allegiance and love.

Peter writes these words about Jesus Christ:

> Although you have not seen him, you love him; and even though you do not see him now, you believe in him and rejoice with an indescribable and glorious joy, for you are receiving the outcome of your faith, the salvation of your souls.—1 Peter 1:8-9

Receiving the presence of Christ is receiving Christ himself—the selfsame one who lived, died, and rose again. But now his presence is invisible to our natural eyes because these eyes can see only what is finite. Christ is now infinite, unlimited, eternal, and cosmic. Such reality cannot be contained, controlled, or confined. But such reality can be received. We receive Christ

> in simplicity—like a child
> in sincerity—like a seeker
> in surrender—like a lover

John writes, "He was in the world, and the world came into being through him; yet the world did not know him. He came to what was his own, and his own people did not accept him. But to all who received him, who believed in his name, he gave power to become children of God" (John 1:10-12). Today, Christ still comes to us, but we often do not recognize him. But we can welcome Christ into our lives, into the deepest part of ourselves, the center of our being. This welcome is not like a business transaction but more like a loving kiss or warm embrace. Christ uses the language of receiving a friend or loved one into our home as a metaphor for faith: "'Listen! I am standing at the door, knocking; if you hear my voice and open the door, I will come in to you and eat with you, and you with me'" (Rev. 3:20).

To receive Christ is simple, but it may not be easy because it assumes a recognition of our need. And we who think of ourselves as strong and self-sufficient find it humbling to admit that we are not. There is so much that we do not know and cannot know. And no matter how much we achieve, accumulate, or accomplish, we are finite, limited, and vulnerable.

We also hate to admit we are weak, frail, and broken. It is hard for us to act like a child who has little pretense or little resistance to wonder and mystery. Yet if we are to receive Christ, we do so like a child. On more than one occasion Jesus commended a child-like spirit. "He called a child, whom he put among them, and said, 'Truly I tell you, unless you change and become like children, you will never enter the kingdom of heaven. Whoever becomes humble like this child is the greatest in the kingdom of heaven'" (Matt. 18:2-4).

A child intuitively and instinctively trusts, welcomes, and receives love, whereas most of us are counterintuitive and calculating. We find it difficult to open our hearts, minds, and spirits and to receive what is freely and simply offered. In great love God offers us this unspeakable gift in Christ.

The First Christian

The first person to receive Christ in her life was his mother, Mary. Now to be sure, hers was a unique and special role in history. She literally bore Christ's body in her body. Yet her simple, profound faith stands as a powerful model for us and as an example of what it means to receive Christ.

> The angel said to her, "Do not be afraid, Mary, for you have found favor with God. And now, you will conceive in your womb and bear a son, and you will name him Jesus. He will be great, and will be called the Son of the Most High, and the Lord God will give to him the throne of his ancestor David. He will reign

over the house of Jacob forever, and of his kingdom there will be no end." Mary said to the angel, "How can this be, since I am a virgin?" The angel said to her, "The Holy Spirit will come upon you, and the power of the Most High will overshadow you; therefore the child to be born will be holy; he will be called Son of God. . . ." Then Mary said,

> *"Here am I, the servant of the Lord;*
> *let it be with me according to your word."*

Then the angel departed from her.—Luke 1:30-35, 38 (italics added)

Here we witness the essence of faith. First comes surprise. The appearance and announcement of the angel is unexpected, and the angel's offer is impossible from a human, rational point of view. So it is with us: we are offered the opportunity for Christ to be born in us and to live in us—not in the same way as with Mary but in a way just as real and just as life-changing. And the offer itself is a surprise. It comes to us as a wonder—a beautiful and amazing possibility.

Immediately we confront the decision whether we will say "yes" or "no" or "not yet" or "I can't" or "that's impossible" or "I'm afraid of what this can mean." Mary's responded clearly,

> *"Here am I, the servant of the Lord;*
> *let it be with me according to your word."*

Mary shows us the way by modeling how to receive Christ and continue to receive Christ. Say yes to the surprise, yes to the mystery, yes to the word of the Lord, but most of all, yes to the One who wants to make his home within us.

No two people receive the presence of Christ in exactly the same way. Some of us are extroverted, while others are introverted. Some of us are rational; others are more emotional. Each of us perceives and processes reality in ways unique to our personality. And it is a mistake to prescribe one form, one method, one rule or one ritual that enables all to receive Christ in the same way.

This truth is clear: the presence of Christ is a gift. It is offered freely to anyone and to everyone. Just as God's creation is a gift and God's love is a gift and eternal life is a gift, so the living and abiding presence of Jesus Christ is a gift.

Status is not important. Past religious performance is not necessary. Worthiness is not the issue. Perfection is not required. But what is required is a receptive and open heart—a simple capacity to trust and to accept what is offered.

The First Easter

> After the sabbath, as the first day of the week was dawning, Mary Magdalene and the other Mary went to see the tomb. And suddenly there was a great earthquake; for an angel of the Lord, descending from heaven, came and rolled back the stone and sat on it. His appearance was like lightning, and his clothing was white as snow. For fear of him the guards shook and became like dead men. But the angel said to the women, "Do not be afraid; I know that you are looking or Jesus who was crucified. He is not here; for he has been raised, as he said. Come, see the place where he lay."—Matthew 28:1-6

With the resurrection of Jesus God marks a new beginning for humanity. Jesus did not return to the earthly order in which he had lived. Nor did the resurrection restore the physical existence destroyed by death. Rather it was the translation of Jesus into a transcendent yet tangible life completely new to human experience.

The risen Christ is the same Christ as before death, yet he is not the same. The nail prints still in his hands signify a continuity of personality and identity, but at the same time a radical discontinuity cannot be denied. No longer is Jesus limited by time and space as we know them. The life he shares with God is a kind of life and reality that can only be described by the word *eternal*.

Resurrection comes as a surprise. It cannot be explained. It defies rationality and leaves us in wonder and amazement. God did what humanity thought impossible. God worked in a way that simply cannot be verified by natural criteria. The resurrection of Jesus is miracle and mystery that results in more questions than answers. But one thing is certain. Resurrection is the great reversal that stands everything on its head. It challenges and changes what we thought we knew. And it definitely changes us.

> When it was evening on that day, the first day of the week, and the doors of the house where the disciples had met were locked for fear of the Jews, Jesus came and stood among them and said, "Peace be with you." After he said this, he showed them his hands and his side. Then the disciples rejoiced when they saw the Lord.—John 20:19-22

Can you imagine what these disciples were feeling that first Easter night? Surely they felt fear that what had happened to Jesus would happen to them. I also think the disciples felt shame and guilt. They had failed Jesus. They knew they had forsaken him, left him and let him die alone. And they had to feel great guilt, great unworthiness.

No doubt they also felt anger. Their beloved Lord had been crucified, and they knew the ones responsible for his crucifixion had acted unjustly. They were angry. And Jesus stepped into this room of frightened, shamed, angry disciples to say, "Peace be with you."

These disciples reflect the universal human experience. As I look within me and around me, I see so much fear, so much guilt, and so much anger. We all struggle with what the desert fathers called "the passions," those patterns of behavior that keep us from loving God and loving neighbor. We are plagued and sometimes paralyzed by these passions, and we desperately need to receive the presence and peace of Christ.

I was deeply affected by the death of Pope John Paul II. And in listening to a televised interview with Zbigniew Brzezinski, the national security advisor under President Carter, I was struck by how Brzezinski described the pope as having a great inner serenity. He could sit quietly in the midst of great conflict, dissenting opinions, intense pressure, and listen with a nonanxious presence. Isn't this what we need? An inner calm? A blessed assurance? A quiet center? Christ offers us his peace by offering his presence.

Christ's Presence	CALMS OUR FEARS
	CLEANSES OUR GUILT
	COOLS OUR ANGER

When Christ breathed on the disciples and said to them, "Receive the Holy Spirit," it was surely a foretaste of that event that would happen fifty days later when God poured out the Holy Spirit on the Day of Pentecost. The gift of the Spirit is the gift of Christ's presence in every believer, in all believers. Christ is not just up there, or out there, or back there. Now Christ can be present with us and within us.

I remember a simple refrain that I sang in church as a small boy that captures the essence of where it all begins:

> Come into my heart, Lord Jesus
> Come in today
> Come in to stay,
> Come into my heart, Lord Jesus.[1]

Reflection Questions

Receiving the presence of Christ is like illumination or inspiration. However frail or fallen we may be, if we desire the presence of Christ, we need only say yes, and it comes. Christ comes.

1. Describe the beginnings of your relationship with Jesus Christ. Which of the following phrases describe the experience of receiving Christ into your life? Why?

   > Like fire
   > Like water
   > Like light
   > Like morning after the dark night
   > Like a friend I've always known but never known
   > Like a lover who has found a beloved
   > Like a parent welcoming a wayward child
   > Like a mother embracing a baby

2. Read again Luke 1:30-35, 38 (on pages 20–21), Mary's experience of "receiving Christ." What similarities to her experience do you find in your life? What differences?

3. Do you consider Christian conversion an event or a process? a one-time experience or a lifelong experience? How does your perception of conversion affect your Christian discipleship?

CHAPTER 2

The Basics
Nurturing the Presence
of Christ

Just as lungs must always be receiving air to breathe, eyes always receiving light to see, and ears always receiving sound to hear, so our spirit must always be receiving love to live. We will never reach a time when we will not need the rush and flow God's love made real by the presence of Christ.

Nurturing the Presence through Love

The good news Jesus Christ revealed is that God loves us. Jesus lived, taught, and died to show that the Creator God, the Covenant-making God, the Holy God, the only God loves us. Jesus showed us that God loves us like a mother who cares for her baby. God loves us like a father who welcomes home a prodigal son. God loves us like a lover who pursues his or her beloved. God's love for us goes beyond a general benevolence or good will toward all humanity. God's love is highly personal for each human being—individualized, intimate, and passionate.

God in love is always pursuing us, reaching out to us, desiring to bless us. God in love is inexhaustible and endless in a desire to have a personal relationship with us, to be our source and strength, to be our Savior and Sustainer. And this love does not depend on our performance of good works or our worthiness to receive it. God's love flows from God's own character as gracious and compassionate.

We were created in love and for love, and when we receive the living presence of Christ into our lives, we are receiving the pure and perfect love of God. We are taking into our deepest selves that for which we were created. Just as the lungs can receive air, the eyes can receive light, and the ears can receive sound, so our spirit can receive love.

And just as lungs must always be receiving air to breathe, eyes always receiving light to see, and ears always receiving sound to hear, so our spirit must always be receiving love to live. We will never reach a time when we will not need the rush and flow God's love made real by the presence of Christ.

What is the most elemental and essential characteristic of our humanity? the deepest point of personality? the center of our being? Some would say it is our reason and rationality. Others would say our ability to feel emotion. Still others would contend that the will and capacity to choose define us. All these attributes are surely components of what it means to be human—and also to be made in the image of God. But I would suggest that the most fundamental component of our humanity is the human spirit. It is God-breathed, and it animates mind, emotion, and will. The divine Spirit bears witness in and to our spirit. And when our spirit is awakened, we are able to discern and experience the love of God.

To be human involves more than becoming a highly evolved or developed species with the capacity to think, feel, and act. To be human is to be endowed by the eternal Spirit with the spiritual capacity to receive God's love, experience God's love, and enjoy God's love. Unlike angels, we are bodily beings; but unlike animals, we are spirit beings. We are more than flesh and blood, neutrons and nerve endings. We are fearfully and wonderfully made as living, breathing sons and daughters of God, who is Spirit. At our center we are spirit capable of love.

The final words Jesus spoke on the cross were, "Father, into your hands I commend my spirit" (Luke 23:46). That statement was a beautiful prayer of faith and release, and it is also a beautiful example for us to follow, not only in death but in all of life. We can surrender our spirit to the will and love of God. We can ask that God not only receive our spirit but communicate with us in our spirit. And God will do just that. God will give us a personal spiritual relationship that will consume and transform us.

In this relationship, our mind will be fully engaged with rational and rigorous thought. Our emotions will soar and sense the true and the beautiful. We will be even more morally responsible, seeking the good and choosing the right because we will have found our center.

The letter we read to early Christians in Ephesus expresses the potential of inner growth in the Spirit:

> I pray that, according to the riches of his glory, he may grant that you may be strengthened in your inner being with power through his Spirit, and that Christ may dwell in your hearts through faith, as you are being rooted and grounded in love. I pray that you may have the power to comprehend, with all the saints, what is the breadth and length and height and depth, and to know the love of Christ that surpasses knowledge, so that you may be filled with all the fullness of God.—Ephesians 3:16-19

I am convinced that the reason so many of us have so little of God's love to offer others is because we know so little of God's love in ourselves. We cannot give someone else what we do not experience. Our hearts are hard and our spirits are cold. Only when we are "rooted and grounded in love" can we give love. Only when we "have the power to comprehend" this love can we share it freely. Only when we "know the love of Christ" can we be instruments and vessels to those around us.

Nurturing the Presence through the Scriptures

After his resurrection, the living Christ appeared to two disciples on the road to Emmaus. They were saddened and distraught by the events of recent days. They did not recognize Jesus and did not understand all that had happened. He rebuked them for being "foolish" and "slow of heart to believe all that the prophets have declared" (Luke 24:25). Then he did something quite remarkable, "Beginning with Moses and all the prophets, he interpreted to them the things about himself in all the Scriptures" (Luke 24:27).

Wouldn't it be wonderful to hear the living Christ do for us what he did for these disciples. Well, we can, because the living Christ wants us to listen to him and learn of him from the pages of the Bible. This means that we can open the Bible to hear from the living Christ and learn the living Christ. So if we want to nurture the presence of Christ, we can and should come often to scriptures with the sincere desire to learn.

Learn the Story

Once I saw a movie in which the opening credits created the sense that the viewer was reading a book. The graphics showed a hand turning page after page, and I read the words written on the pages as they went by. All at once the words on the pages morphed into screen images: the story unfolded out of the book. That visual sequence illustrates my view of the Bible: a living story unfolds out of the pages of the Bible. And the central character in that story is Jesus Christ.

The Bible records many fascinating stories, but all the stories of the Bible comprise one great story, one unfolding drama, one grand epic. It is a narrative of God's self-revelation in history beginning with the creation of the universe and the choice of Abraham as the father of Israel. The story unfolds with an account of the Hebrew people and continues with the ministry of Christ and the expansion of the early church. Out of the pages of scripture a story emerges. As I read and reflect on the story, the central character becomes real to me. From the words on the page, inspired by the Spirit, comes the living Word. Just as a thought is expressed in a word, Jesus Christ as the expression of God is the living Word. And so I read the Bible to receive the living Word—not only to receive this Word but also to be transformed by it.

We nurture the presence of Christ by learning the story. Then we face the opportunity to enter into the story personally. In other words, when we read the Bible, we can put ourselves in the story. I become the prodigal son, Nicodemus, Zacchaeus. The story of my life and the story of the Bible become one. I enter into the characters of the Bible, and they enter into me.

The great truths of the Bible describe and define me. These ideas of creation, sin, and salvation are not just classical ideas or abstract doctrines but the narrative of my life. And the God of the Bible becomes real to me. The God of Abraham, Isaac, and Jacob becomes my God. The God and Father of our Lord Jesus Christ becomes my father. Everything in the Bible proceeds from the story. Everything we call theology or ethics or principles exists in the context of God's unfolding story. The first part leads to the last parts. The Old gives way to the New. So as I read, study, and meditate on the Bible, I'm caught up in the story and become a part of what God has done and is doing in history.

LEARN THE TRUTH

Jesus had significant encounters with the scribes and Pharisees throughout his ministry. These men intensely devoted to scripture not only believed scripture to be divinely inspired but also studied and applied it in minute detail. Yet Jesus strongly rebuked these religious leaders: "You search the scriptures because you think that in them you have eternal life; and it is they that testify on my behalf" (John 5:39).

The Pharisees failed to understand that the written Word of God bears witness to the Living Word of God and that truth is to be found in a trusting, loving devotion to the Living Word, that is, in a relationship. Adherence to human-created creeds, legalistic obedience to rules, or strict observance of ritual will not lead to truth. But sincere faith and simple obedience to the One whom scripture calls "Faithful and True" (Rev. 19:11) leads to truth.

When Jesus was standing before Pilate, Pilate asked, "So you are a king?" to which Jesus answered, "You say that I am a king. For this I was born, and for this I came into the world, to testify to the truth. Everyone who belongs to the truth listens to my voice" (John 18:37). Everything about Jesus testifies to truth. His words are true; his deeds of mercy are true; and his example of compassion and justice are true. He embodies truth.

And yet it is possible for someone to look right at the truth and not believe, not love, not follow, and therefore not understand truth. This is what Pilate did. He asked Jesus, "What is truth?" (John 18:38). Jesus did not answer. If Pilate did not recognize the One standing in front of him as truth, no amount of logic or debate could change him. Only in receiving the One who is truth, can truth be experienced.

The Bible is a library of books. Its various genres include law, prophecy, wisdom, gospel, history, and poetry, but the central character in this library of historical documents is God as revealed in Jesus Christ. When I read the Bible, my desire is to receive Christ, to learn of Christ, to know Christ through these various books. I don't read the Bible just to get information or to learn facts (although such reading has a place). Instead, I read the Bible to nurture a relationship with Christ.

Nurturing the Presence through Silence

Many of us cannot hear the voice of Christ, feel the Spirit of Christ, or nurture the presence of Christ because of life's noises. Silence is, by definition, the absence of noise—no conversation, no music, no distractions from calendars or clocks; no pressure from work or play; just stillness.

More than these absences, though, silence can be a disposition, an attitude, a perspective. Often the greatest noise we experience comes not from what other people create nor from machines but from within—the noisy clatter of guilt, shame, fear, and anger. Internal voices shout at us, and sometimes we scream back. One can be all alone yet not enter into silence.

Silence itself must be created, nurtured, cultivated. It doesn't just happen. But if a person wants to follow Jesus, he or she must be willing to follow Jesus into times of silence. While on earth, Jesus often spent time in silence and solitude. He went into the desert for forty days. He spent entire nights alone in prayer. He rose early to be alone. He retreated from the crowds, the disciples, and the human need that everywhere pressed upon him. Jesus practiced silence.

Jesus commanded us, "Whenever you pray, do not be like the hypocrites; for they love to stand . . . at the street corners. . . . But whenever you pray, go into your room and shut the door and pray to your Father who is in secret" (Matt. 6:5-6). Silence is secret in that it is it hidden from others and also hidden in the private parts of our own heart. Silence is known only to the one who practices it. And while silence is a secret space, it is also a sacred space, a kind of holy of holies.

Make no mistake, however, silence can be terrifying. Perhaps we avoid it for that reason; we do anything and everything but go there. Silence can be terrifying because we will encounter our own selves. Not the false self that we create and project to others but the true self that God creates. Silence has a way of stripping away our pretenses and illusions, exposing our finitude and mortality. It also has a way of causing us to encounter God: not a false god created and controlled by us but the true God who is holy mystery. Some have been known to weep or tremble at such an encounter.

But as frightening as it seems, silence actually renews and recreates. In it we are healed and energized. In it we discover gifts and treasures otherwise hidden. So let me invite you to enter times of silence. Do not be afraid. To hear the voice of Christ and nurture the presence of Christ, be silent.

Nurturing the Presence through Letting Go

Mary of Bethany offers us a beautiful and profound model of how to nurture the presence of Christ. Along with her sister, Martha, and her brother, Lazarus, she seems to have had an especially close friendship with Jesus during his ministry. On three separate occasions we get a glimpse of her faith. On the first occasion, she and her sister have invited Jesus into their home, and while Martha prepares the meal, Mary sits at the feet of Jesus, learning from him (see Luke 10:38-42). On another occasion, Lazarus has died, and in great grief Mary falls at the feet of Jesus to say, "Lord, if you had been here, my brother would not have died" (John 11:32). On a third occasion, Mary anoints the feet of Jesus with expensive perfume as an act of devotion and worship (see John 12:1-8). On all three occasions, Mary of Bethany is positioned *at the feet of Jesus.*

In each of these poignant events, the posture of Mary's body indicates an attitude and disposition of her spirit: abandonment to Christ. In every instance she positions herself to wait and worship. She positions herself before Christ in an attitude of surrender. Even when troubled over the death of her brother and Jesus' delay in coming to his rescue, she releases her grief and confusion to Christ. She lets go.

These three situations present a good mental image of what we can do. We can put ourselves and picture ourselves at the feet of Jesus. Like Mary, we can sit at his feet to receive instruction, truth, and enlightenment. We can fall at his feet to receive comfort for our grief and confusion. We can kneel at Jesus' feet in adoration and affection.

Being "at the feet of Christ" is a metaphor, but it is an especially powerful metaphor for those who live in a self-sufficient culture. We who pride ourselves on being self-made or self-reliant have difficulty putting ourselves at anybody's feet. We who want to be in control have difficulty recognizing we are not in control and assuming the mental and spiritual posture of being at the feet of the One who is in control. We who have compulsions and addictions have difficulty letting go and releasing those compulsions and addictions. We who find our identity and worth in *doing* have difficulty in *receiving*.

If it helps, we can use an icon or a picture of Christ to stir the imagination. Or we can read this biblical text and imagine ourselves in Mary's posture and place, or sit with the mental image of ourselves at the feet of Christ. In that posture, we simply let go. We can let go of our pride or fear, our grief or anger. We can release to the God who loves us whatever troubles or confuses us. We can abandon ourselves into the care and providence of the One who desires only our good. We can trust and we can wait.

Reflection Questions

1. In this chapter you read the statement: "I am convinced that the reason so many of us have so little of God's love to offer others is because we know so little of God's love in ourselves." Who or what helps you know and experience God's love more fully? How does knowing God's love for you translate to loving others in your life?

2. What scripture passages make Christ come alive to you, nurturing your sense of Christ's presence in your life? Think about what these passages say to you.

3. What has been your experience of silence? What is the place of silence in your Christian practice at this point?

CHAPTER 3

Prayer

Practicing the Presence of Christ

It's not enough to read about prayer or study the lives of saints or have theological conversation about spiritual practices. We learn to pray by praying.

Prayer is both an act and an attitude. We pray in response to the reality of the Triune God by paying attention or by being attentive. God is always present and attentive to us, always pursuing, blessing, and loving us. God is always reaching out to offer grace and goodness to us. God is inexhaustible and unrelenting in pure pursuit and presence.

Prayer is then our attentiveness to God. It enables us to live in this presence and to engage in actions that keep us responsive and attentive. We often speak of prayer as conversation, communication, or communion with God, and this is true. But for me, the word *prayer* describes what Brother Lawrence called "the practice the presence of God."[1]

Rule and Rhythm

No one way of prayer fits everybody. The history of Christian spirituality reveals great variety in ways of prayer. Different emphases and even disagreement about praying show up in Christian literature over time. That fact should not discourage us but highlight the reality that many streams flow into what becomes the river of prayer.

There is no one way to categorize or summarize prayer practices, but I want to frame the following conversation about prayer practices in four broad areas:

- body prayer
- vocal prayer
- mental prayer
- contemplative prayer

Because each of us is unique in temperament, circumstances, and experience, we cannot name any universal rule or rhythm for the practice of prayer. And on our journey we go through stages that require adjustment to any rule or rhythm we adopt. But let it be clear that each of us does need to establish a pattern of discipline for prayer practices. If we do not create some order and organization for prayer, our sincere desires will be only wishful longings. Prayer practices are just what they say—*practices* that require performance. Without coercion, each individual must determine a "rule of life" or daily discipline. It's not enough to read about prayer or study the lives of saints or have theological conversation about spiritual practices. We learn to pray by praying.

In similar fashion, the rhythm of our lives will vary. I prefer the word *rhythm* to *balance* because life is an ongoing story. Life never stops, and it is never static.[2] The story of our life unfolds continuously—yearly, monthly, daily, hourly. So we will always be learning the practices of prayer. But we need a holy rhythm incorporating work and play, solitude and community, family and ministry, engagement and retreat, activity and rest. The practices of prayer fit into that rhythm. They complement that rhythm and enrich it.

BODY PRAYER

Since we are bodily creatures, everything we do in some way involves physicality. Using our body as a response to God constitutes body prayer. Subjecting the body to a regimen for spiritual purposes is to engage our physical self for spiritual ends. This can be a powerful practice.

Fasting is one form of body prayer. To fast is to deprive the body of something in order to become conscious of the presence of Christ. This intentional act of physical self-denial heightens awareness and attentiveness. Jesus himself seems to have approved of fasting as a spiritual discipline, although he had some strong words of instruction for those who practice it. Fasting is to be performed for God alone with no thought of public recognition or praise from other people (see Matt. 6:16-18).

A regimen of physical activity or physical exercise can surely be a form of body prayer. I know individuals who walk or run daily "to the glory of God," with the specific aim of spiritual as well as physical health. An Orthodox monk once described to me his daily discipline of genuflecting, bowing, and prostrating himself. I was amazed by the devotion and intensity of these acts. Even a regular "sit" in Centering Prayer requires physical self-control, and anyone who has tried it, knows how difficult it can be. Sometimes the body doesn't want to be still.

Indeed it seems that the body at times has "a mind of its own" and does not want to be controlled. Instead, it wants to be in control. However, the body can be commandeered and commanded in the worship of God. It can be a vehicle for embodying and expressing praise, confession, or petition.

What is the appropriate bodily posture for prayer? Of course the answer is that there is no one appropriate posture. But neither is bodily posture irrelevant or unimportant in prayer. One ancient posture for prayer is lying prostrate on the floor—face down with arms outstretched. We may find this practice too radical because we pamper our body and treasure it too highly. In stark contrast, the apostle Paul speaks of punishing his body and enslaving it "so that after proclaiming to others I myself should not be disqualified" (1 Cor. 9:27). This text has been misused by people who inflicted pain on their body thinking it would make them more spiritual. Today we typically face the opposite problem: our disconnect between body and spirit makes it strange or embarrassing to speak of lying on the floor in worship.

A more modest posture might be bowing in prayer—to bow down low as a sign of humility and reverence. Most of us can manage to bow our head as a gesture of worship, but to bow down from the waist or to bow down in a kneeling position feels strange to some. I have fond memories of my father who was not ashamed to kneel and pray. Yet I am sad to say that I grew up in a faith tradition where I seldom saw anyone kneel or bow in corporate worship. The psalmist invites us to do just that.

> O come, let us worship and bow down,
>   let us kneel before the LORD, our Maker!
> For he is our God,
>   and we are the people of his pasture,
>   and the sheep of his hand.—Psalm 95:6-7

Indeed the apostle Paul quotes Isaiah:

> For it is written,
> "As I live, says the Lord, every knee shall bow to me,
>   and every tongue shall give praise to God."
> —Romans 14:11

You might experiment with a variety of bodily postures. Try standing as the Christian Orthodox do and swaying as some Orthodox Jews do and dancing as some Pentecostals do. If you kneel, bow, walk, sit, and even prostrate yourself on the floor, your body can, over a period of time, be fully engaged in prayer.

If, however, all this sounds too exhausting, consider the use of our hands as a way to practice the presence of Christ. For centuries, many Christians have made the sign of the cross as an act of devotion. Others have clasped or cupped their hands together as a form of silent prayer, while still others have clapped with their hands in a kind of applause or celebration before God. Both in the Old and New Testaments, we are encouraged to lift our hands in worship (Ps. 28:2; 63:4; 1 Tim. 2:8), with the clear instruction that they are to be "holy hands." Whether an upturned palm or an extended and upraised arm, gesturing with hands represents an ancient prayer practice.

Other bodily prayers include gently kissing a treasured object, such as a Bible or prayer book; offering a "breath prayer" that synchronizes breathing with words; and intentional, restful relaxation as a way to express faith. Learning to be attentive to God with the body in any or all these ways is a liberating experience.

VOCAL PRAYER

In vocal prayer we use our voice in some way as a response to God. Vocal prayer is probably the most common and widely accepted way to practice the presence of Christ. We use our voice in both private and public prayers to capture and convey thought or convey emotion toward God. Even reading and writing a prayer represents a form of vocal prayer.

In scripture we read of many times when people "called on the Lord" in some way. They said a prayer with their lips. Their voice was heard, and someone recorded what was heard. Jesus instructed his disciples, "When you pray, say . . ." (Luke 11:2). Jesus himself offered vocal prayers to God. "In the days of his flesh, Jesus offered up prayers and supplications, with loud cries and tears" (Heb. 5:7). On one occasion, we are told, Jesus was praying and when he had finished, one of his disciples asked him, "Lord, teach us to pray"

(Luke 11:1). No doubt it was an amazing experience to hear Jesus voice prayers to his Father.

Wouldn't you love to have heard Jesus pray? Of all that Jesus did during his earthly life, I would love to have heard him pray. It would have been remarkable to listen to him teach and preach or to watch him perform miracles or cast out demons. But to have listened to the vocal prayer of Jesus would have been an experience like no other.

Actually scripture reveals very little content of Jesus' prayers with the exception of the High Priestly Prayer in John 17. All other recorded prayers of Jesus are brief and poignant. Yet it seems logical to conclude that as an observant Jew, Jesus voiced the customary prayers at morning, noon, and night; at meals and at festivals. He knew and loved the Hebrew scriptures and no doubt recited the prayers of the Psalms. From his teachings we know of his identity and intimacy with God, whom he called Father. This relationship must have influenced his conversation and communion with God as did his self-understanding.

To put it plainly, Jesus was a man of prayer. He prayed earnestly and often. In addition to observing the traditions of Jewish prayer practice, he rose early to pray. He retreated regularly from the multitudes and even from his disciples, just to pray. At times he spent an entire night in prayer. Before, during, and after significant events in his ministry, he prayed. Jesus spent the first thirty years of his life in obscurity, years when he learned to pray. During his public ministry, he showed us that prayer was essential and integral to him, and he taught prayer to his disciples. Jesus practiced prayer throughout his life and even as he was dying. Surely this life of prayer involved more than vocal prayer but clearly included it.

We learn from Jesus—both from his teachings and his example—why and how to have conversation with God. As audacious as it may sound, we can talk with as well as listen to the Creator of the universe. Here then are several different forms of vocal prayer, ways to practice the presence of Christ.

We can TALK to God. Using the ordinary words of our everyday life, we can speak in and to God's presence. We need not adapt religious vocabulary or learn a code language. We do not need to speak in a sanctified tone or use theological words. We can use the same verbiage and vocabulary that we use with our family and friends in the everyday commerce of life. In talking to and with God, we can use our "heart language"—being honest and transparent. We surely do not inform God with our prayers, so we can speak frankly, sharing those thoughts, hurts, fears, and insecurities we keep from everyone.

We can SING to God. Commands and exhortations to voice our prayers to God in music fill the scriptures. Some people can sing a prayer better than they can say it. Others have difficulty with this form of expression, not because of musical deficiency but because of spiritual deficiency. There's no melody in their heart. We can voice our prayers and praise in song even if the sound is not pleasing to other people.

We can CHANT to God. A form of vocal prayer that may or may not be musical is the chant. Contrary to what some say, chanting need not be the "vain repetitions" Jesus condemned. Rather it can be a sincere and serious repetition of a word, phrase, or song that feeds and focuses the spirit on Christ. Listening to a chant may also provide the means to practice the presence of Christ.

We can SHOUT to God. This is an often repeated admonition in the Psalms (see 33:3; 35:27; 47:1). Although it may seem strange to some, a shout indicates intensity, passion, and fervor in the pursuit of the holy. I've experienced a wonderful example of this expression in the Korean church where simultaneous congregational shouting is a regular ritual in public worship.

We can WHISPER to God. In contrast to the shout is the whisper, perhaps even an inaudible whisper. The best biblical example of this practice is Hannah who prayed in the presence of Eli, the priest: "As she continued praying before the LORD, Eli observed her mouth. Hannah was praying silently; only her lips moved, but her voice was not heard" (1 Sam. 1:12-13). I remember a simple chorus sung often when I was a boy:

> Whisper a prayer in the morning,
> Whisper a prayer at noon,
> Whisper a prayer in the evening,
> To keep your heart in tune.

We can GROAN to God. When words are inadequate to express emotion or speak a response, we can turn to this form of vocal prayer. All we can do is sigh or vent with an inarticulate utterance. The apostle Paul speaks of the groan of creation, the groan of the human heart, and the groan of the Spirit (see Rom. 8:22-23, 26, NIV). Surely all these can be both expressed and heard.

We can LAMENT or LAUGH to God. These two practices express opposite emotions, and both are valid. The lament verbally expresses a complaint and conveys anger, grief, and confusion in the presence of God. Numerous Psalms are laments, and of course the Book of Lamentation is a psalter of communal grief. Jesus himself practiced this form of prayer in his grief over Jerusalem (see Matt. 23:37-39) and in his cry of dereliction from the cross, a lament from Psalm 22. Jesus gives us a model to follow.

Laughter, a spontaneous sign of gladness, offers medicine for the spirit. The psalmist shows how this practice can express joy to God,

> When the LORD restored the fortunes of Zion,
>   we were like those who dream.
> Then our mouth was filled with laughter,
>   and our tongue with shouts of joy.—Psalm 126:1-2

We can BABBLE to God. The gift of a prayer language is a vocal expression for many Christians. Sometimes called "speaking in tongues" or "glossolalia," the practice is prominent in Pentecostal, charismatic churches. This practice, like any other, may not be the experience of everyone, but it has been meaningful to many.

MENTAL PRAYER

When we frame a thought or construct a mental image in response to God, we engage in mental prayer. We usually think such thoughts or create such images with unspoken words. The thoughts and words are inseparable. The idea and expression are a unity. This mental process becomes an act of prayer when it is God-directed and God-conscious. Often someone will say, "You are in my thoughts and prayers," suggesting that the two are not necessarily the same. One can have a thought of concern that is not a prayer, but a prayer is also a thought.

Some contend that this kind of mental process is only that, a mental process; we are thinking and imaging to ourselves. Because no one can see God or prove God, they reason, attributing anything more to such mental activity is foolish or illusory. While some people may follow this line of reasoning, Christians affirm that prayer is an act of faith. There may be good evidence that "prayer changes things," or we may have witnessed "answered prayer," but in the final analysis, prayer is not a scientific exercise. It is a faith exercise. C. S. Lewis offers the following explanation:

The question then arises, "What sort of evidence *would* prove the efficacy of prayer?" The thing we pray for may happen, but how can you ever know it was not going to happen anyway? Even if the thing were indisputably miraculous it would not follow that the miracle had occurred because of your prayers. The answer surely is that a compulsive empirical proof such as we have in the sciences can never be attained.

Some things are proved by the unbroken uniformity of our experiences. The law of gravitation is established by the fact that, in our experience, all bodies without exception obey it. Now even if all the things that people prayed for happened, which they do not, this would not prove what Christians mean by the efficacy of prayer. For prayer is request. The essence of request as distinct from compulsion, is that it may or may not be granted."[3]

Hebrews 11:1 says, "Now faith is the assurance of things hoped for, the conviction of things not seen." Prayer has to do with the God we cannot see, prove, or explain. Prayer has to do with a reality we long for, hope for, and yearn for. Hebrews 11:6 then says, "And without faith it is impossible to please God, for whoever would approach him must believe that he exists and that he rewards those who seek him." In prayer we think and talk as if God is really there, and we act as if that God is personal, caring, and responsive.

Whenever we speak of prayer, we use analogy, symbol, and metaphor to speak of a reality beyond thought and word. We describe prayer as "coming into the presence," yet we are always in the presence of God. We describe prayer as "approaching God," yet it is God who approaches us. We do not literally "come before God's throne"—whether of grace or glory; rather God is spirit who is at all places and at all times. God is not just "out there" or "up there" but is "in here" as well.

Even speaking of God in the masculine gender misrepresents the incomprehensible nature of God. God is neither male nor female but wholly other and the holy other. Our language, like our knowledge, is limited. We refer to prayer as talking with God, and yet some of the most sublime forms of prayer do not involve words. While our language about prayer is symbolic, behind the symbol lies the pure act of believing that God is, that God cares, that God is involved in our lives, and that a personal relationship with God is possible. Prayer, especially mental prayer, is paying attention or fixing our thoughts or centering our lives on "the unvisible" reality we call God.

Discourse

People most frequently practice the form of mental prayer we would call conversation. We form a mental construct and express it to God, believing that God hears and answers. We are speaking, if only mentally, and God is listening. Jesus offered the disciples a model prayer in this style. This model instructs us how to have discourse and conversation with God.

> Our Father in heaven,
>   hallowed be your name.
>   Your kingdom come.
>   Your will be done,
>   on earth as it is in heaven.
>   Give us this day our daily bread.
>   And forgive us our debts,
>   as we also have forgiven our debtors.
>   And do not bring us to the time of trial,
>   but rescue us from the evil one.—Matthew 6:9-13

The opening line, "Our Father in heaven, hallowed be your name," tells us we may address God directly. Of the many biblical names for God, I find none more beautiful than "Father," the idea of God as a heavenly parent. I remember receiving a particular phone call from one of my children. When I answered the phone and heard the voice say, "Hi, Dad," I immediately smiled with pleasure because I recognized the voice of my child. In a similar yet greater way, God is pleased when we pray. Always God wants us to pray and to turn our thoughts heavenward.

"Hallowed be your name. Your kingdom come, your will be done." In all our discourse we are to revere God as the Holy One, always surrendering to the divine will and seeking the divine order of reality. We should offer our thoughts toward God in an attitude of humble seeking and submission. Whatever else we may ask or say should be done in the attitude of worship and adoration. Our first and most important request should always be for the kingdom and will of God to come.

"Give us this day our daily bread." We can ask for what we truly need. Since God is loving Creator and holy parent, we need not hesitate to make our requests known. We can offer God the concerns of life, both for ourselves and for others, with confidence in God's provision for those concerns.

"And forgive us our debts, as we also have forgiven our debtors." We can confess our sins, seeking forgiveness just as we offer forgiveness to those who sin against us. Our guilt, brokenness, and failure are ever with us; and we desperately need salvation and healing. Our constant need is to receive restoration and then become instruments of that restoration to others.

"And do not bring us to the time of trial, but rescue us from the evil one." We can also appeal for protection and rescue from the real evil within us and around us. We can seek guidance and providential help in the awesome struggle with sin. We live in a dangerous world and urgently need divine assistance.

Mental discourse with the living God is a holy and sacred privilege. Whether we turn our thoughts heavenward in praise and thanksgiving, in repentance and contrition, in petition and intercession, we are engaging in one of the great and grand privileges of human existence. To be able to pray is to be human.

Meditation

Meditation is thinking reflectively on a biblical or spiritual truth. It is a cognitive experience in which we hold an idea in the consciousness for a prolonged period of time. Meditation's immediate goal is insight and inspiration. Its long-term goal is transformation, accomplished by internalizing the truth at both the conscious and the subconscious level. In this practice, a person meditates "on" something, focusing the mind on its meaning and value. This quiet process shuts out mental distractions to allow the reality and power of the truth to penetrate the total personality.

We can read numerous biblical accounts of meditation. God told Joshua, "This book of the law shall not depart out of your mouth, you shall meditate on it day and night" (Josh. 1:8). The Psalms reference the value of meditation on the precepts of scripture (see, for example, 1:2; 19:14; 119:15). Mary, the mother of Jesus, after hearing the words and witness of the shepherds, "treasured all these words and pondered them in her heart" (Luke 2:19). After her experience in the Temple, we read, "his mother treasured all these things in her heart" (Luke 2:51). Mary clearly treasured both spoken words and remembered events.

Meditation calls us to ponder and consider at length the word and will of God. It is a reflection, a musing, a thoughtful lingering on a grace gift, a challenge, a promise, an experience. Meditation manifests a trustful, patient waiting before a revealed reality, expecting the spirit to bear fruit within.

Imagination

Mental prayer can take the form of imagination when we put ourselves into a biblical story. In this type of prayer we go beyond understanding scripture factually or historically and create a mental picture that brings the story to life in our consciousness. This mental effort helps the truth of that story come alive in our behavior.

Much of scripture feeds imagination because it is designed to do so. The poetry of the wisdom literature, the profound words and acts of the Hebrew prophets, the parables of Jesus, all fire the imagination. The apocalyptic literature, particularly the book of Revelation, jumps off the pages to stimulate our thoughts.

Just as the Spirit can instruct and enlighten the rational process, it also can stir the imagination and create a profound response to God. We need not be afraid of an awakened imagination anymore than rational discourse.

Remembering

Mental prayer also includes reflection on the past. To be able to remember is both gift and responsibility. And scripture requires us to practice remembrance. Sacred rituals in both the Old and New Testaments enable the people of faith to remember God's saving act in the past. Humans tend to forget divine providence and the divine promises. So we need to set specific times to remember. One purpose of sabbath is to provide such a time. Indeed, God commands, "Remember the sabbath." Keeping the sabbath is a way to pray.[4] Keeping a journal can be a good aid in remembering, and this too can be a way of praying. Writing down the activities of the day stimulates the memory. The journal then becomes a resource for future reflection. Journaling uses the body and the mind and provides a way to remember and keep inventory.
I remember as a boy singing the hymn,

> Count your many blessings, name them one by one;
>
> . . . .
>
> Count your many blessings, see what God hath done.[5]

The very act of counting or keeping a record is a way of remembering the past. The psalmist speaks of counting as a way of remembering:

> How weighty to me are your thoughts, O God!
> How vast is the sum of them!

I try to count them—they are more than the sand.
—Psalm 139:17-18

It is unclear to me whether the psalmist is trying to count his thoughts toward God or God's thoughts toward him. Either way, the psalmist remembers and prays. Later on in this psalm we read:

Search me, O God, and know my heart;
   test me and know my thoughts.
See if there is any wicked way in me,
   and lead me in the way everlasting.—Psalm 139:23-24

For this prayer to be answered, the psalmist must reflect on past behavior. So, remembering can be not only an act that leads to thanksgiving but also an act that leads to confession. The spiritual exercises of Ignatius require a daily inventory and examen.[6] This honest self-evaluation and self-questioning prompts the memory and creates opportunity for redemption. It helps us see when we were the presence of Christ and when we weren't. It helps motivate us to live out the potential we have in Christ. And as we are redeemed and transformed, we become better able to be the life-changing presence of Christ in our world.

Reflection Questions

1. With which form of prayer do you feel most comfortable? With which form of prayer do you feel most uncomfortable? After reading this chapter, to which prayer practice do you feel led?

2. Describe the rhythm of your prayer discipline. In what ways would you like to change rhythm?

3. The disciples came to Jesus with the request, "Lord, teach us to pray." Chronicle the times and points in your life when in a profound or simple way you felt the desire to make the same request.

CHAPTER 4

Contemplative Prayer
Resting in the
Presence of Christ

There are times when it is good to stop talking, stop think-ing, stop striving, stop everything, and just "be" in the all-pervasive presence of this loving, good, personal, infinite, and transcendent God.

When, in order to respond to God, we still our mental faculties to listen at a deeper level, we are engaging in contemplative prayer. Sometimes called "meditative prayer," "listening prayer," "the prayer of quiet," or "the prayer of rest," this practice focuses on inner silence and on love in its purest form.

There come times in a relationship when words get in the way, or activities seem superfluous. Sometimes we simply need to be still, to wait and let be. Contemplative prayer for a Christian does not deny or negate the physical and mental realities in which we live. These are God's good creation. Neither does contemplative prayer aim at becoming "nothing," being nothing, or entering into nothing. Christian contemplation is based on the firm belief in a personal, loving God. But it is also based on the belief that this loving God is infinite, holy, and eternal. So there are times when it is good to stop talking, stop thinking, stop striving, stop everything, and just "be" in the all-pervasive presence of this loving, good, personal, infinite, and transcendent God.

I wonder if we are afraid of being silent. Do we fear that if we suspend words and thoughts the world will stop or something terrible might happen to us? Will Satan destroy us? In letting go might we lose control and cease to exist? Are we being irresponsible and foolish? Are we afraid that if we practice this kind of prayer, we might discover our falsehoods and pretenses? Maybe our brokenness and vulnerability would be exposed. These fears can seem terrifying, but they should not deter us. God is above us, below us, beside us, and within us. And we know from the revelation of God in Christ that this God loves us. We need not be afraid.

So the purpose of contemplative prayer is to listen, to be loved, and to love. The purpose is not to get what we need or what we think we need but to allow God to commune with us and communicate grace and goodness in the deepest part of our being. We may or may not feel that grace and goodness during the time of contemplative prayer. That's not what is most important. We may even find it difficult to practice contemplative prayer and may experience anything but peace and well-being during the time of prayer. Again, neither our experience or feeling is most important. What is important is the practice itself. Because in the practice, we are acknowledging our need and desire for God's love, our inability to comprehend and control it, and our confidence in its presence and reality.

What results can we expect? Through the centuries those who have heeded the command to "be still and know that I am God" (Ps. 46:10) testify they have experienced just what is promised. They give testimony to a new and different consciousness of God and of God's love. Their enhanced consciousness heightens their mental process and deepens their emotional responses. But this consciousness is not dependent on either. They also give witness to a new clarity about life, death, suffering, and truth. Their lives demonstrate discernment and wisdom as well as strength of character and serenity of spirit.

Kataphatic Prayer

At the risk of oversimplification, let me summarize two forms of contemplative prayer practiced through the years and taught in a vast body of literature. Kataphatic and apophatic prayer have a common goal—to create a space where God can communicate. We all experience the problem of living distracted and divided lives and have difficulty hearing the holy whisper of God. These forms of contemplative prayer help center, still, or quieten the spirit and prepare us to receive God's gift of God's self.

Kataphatic ("with images") spirituality emphasizes the senses as means of grace and vehicles of the Spirit. To respond to God, we employ the senses in much the same way as we use the mind for mental images. The images that the mind or the senses create are not ends in themselves but means to a greater end—communion with God. In kataphatic prayer, we embrace the means, enjoy them, and experience them to the fullest in our desire to love God and be loved by God.

Music can be a vehicle for kataphatic prayer. because music can awaken, calm, or create feeling; it can transport us into another realm of reality. Music is not irrational but beyond rational. It has the power to capture our attention and lead us to experience God in a way that words or thoughts cannot. Transcending time and space, thought and language, music ushers us into the presence of the Holy. Many testify to entering an "unspeakable" serenity and awareness through music.

We know what it means to weep, to tremble, and to laugh in the presence of God because of music. We have worshiped in ecstasy and sat in absolute silence after hearing music. Words and conversation become an intrusion after such a time. Our agendas seem small, our problems petty, and they recede into the background in the aftereffect of what we have heard. Music can be a means of grace.

In a similar fashion, nature can create a response to God in us. Since the natural order is created by God, it gives testimony to the power and beauty of God. "The heavens are telling the glory of God; and the firmament proclaims his handiwork. Day to day pours forth speech, and night to night declares knowledge" (Ps. 19:1-2). Some people find communing with nature an effective way of communing with God. I prefer speaking of *immersing* myself in nature as a way of communing with the God who created nature. I do not believe that nature and God are synonymous, but I do believe nature bears the signature stamp of its Creator. It can lead us to worship. The vastness of the universe shows us the greatness of God.

> O Lord my God! when I in awesome wonder
> consider all the worlds thy hands have made,
> I see the stars, I hear the rolling thunder,
> Thy power throughout the universe displayed.
> Then sings my soul, my Savior God to thee;
> how great thou art; how great thou art!*

The grandeur and complexity of nature humble us and often bring us to silence. In a sense, nature "puts us in our place" by making limits and finitude clear, both in terms of our understanding and our control of the universe. After God speaks to Job and gives him a glimpse of the immensity of the oceans, the order of the sunrise and sunset, the difference between light and darkness, the fierceness of lightning, the origin of rain, the birthing pattern of animals, the flight of birds, and much more, he asked Job the question, "Shall a faultfinder contend with the Almighty? Anyone who

---

*"How Great Thou Art," copyright 1953 S. K. Hine. Assigned to MANNA MUSIC, INC., 35255 Brooten Road, Pacific City, OR 97135. Renewed 1981. All rights reserved. Used by permission.

argues with God must respond" (Job 40:1). Then Job falls silent. He is stilled, and he answers,

> See, I am of small account;
>   what shall I answer you?
>   I lay my hand on my mouth.
>   I have spoken once, and I will not answer.—Job 40:4-5

Nature has this kind of impact on us. But it can also calm and soothe us. Nature can create a sweetness and healing that no logic or language can. The roar of the ocean can get on the inside of us. The babbling of a brook, the chirping of a bird, or the rustling of wind in a tree can renew the spirit. The sight of a sunrise or sunset can become silent therapy. The scent of mountain air or one single flower can invigorate. Nature can be a means of grace and a vehicle of the Spirit that ushers us into consciousness of the divine presence.

Likewise *artistic beauty* can create contemplative response. Since creative ability is given by the creator, what is created can awaken and arouse the human spirit in a way that nothing else does. Both performing arts (such as dance, drama, film) and visual arts (such as painting and sculpture) have profoundly influenced those who worship God. The art itself has often been an act of worship by the artist and offered as a gift to those who would view it, embrace it, or experience it as a way of prayer.

One of the great controversies in church history took place in the eighth and ninth centuries over the use of images in liturgy and worship. The debate concerned whether to use icons—painted images of Christ, Mary, or Christian saints—in devotional practices. What was decided after intense and extended debate was that art, theology, spiritual reflection, and worship are integral to one another. Each represents a human response to divine mystery, and *objects such as icons* "can be the seat of divine power and that this power can be secured through physical contact with a sacred object."[1] Eventually the view that some art forms themselves become sacred and even sacramental emerged. Personally, I am not comfortable with this view, but I do believe that art forms can be aids in worship, vehicles of the Spirit and means of grace, without the objects themselves becoming sacred.

I have a reproduction of Rembrandt's painting *The Return of the Prodigal Son* in my office. After reading Henri Nouwen's book on his experience with this parable and painting, I too began to sit before it in silent reflection and contemplation. Along with other art objects, that painting has become, for me, a window into both truth and beauty incarnated in Jesus Christ. I can and do sit before a crucifix or a stained glassed window or even an icon and consider the truth conveyed through the object or sit in stillness as an expression of my devotion and openness to God.

No practice of kataphatic prayer is more common than observing the memorial meal Jesus instituted the night before his death. Whatever one's theological perspective on the presence of Christ in the Eucharist, the fact is that we eat the bread and drink from the cup. All the senses are involved, as is the mind, the will, the imagination, and the memory. In this act we enter into the most profound mystery of Christ's person and sacrifice as well as our own salvation. Before such a mystery we can only be amazed and grateful.

However often we come to the Lord's Table—and views differ widely on that frequency—one receives, reflects, and remembers. To consider and contemplate the Incarnate Son of God crucified for us is not only an act of faith and obedience but a spiritual experience like no other. The Lord's Supper proclaims the heart of the Gospel and confesses personal devotion as well as participation in the communal body of Christ.

Apophatic Prayer

Apophatic ("without images") spirituality seeks to minimize and even deny the senses and all mental constructs so as to respond to God alone. The goal of apophatic prayer is response to God rather than our thoughts or feelings about God or images of God. Sometimes called "desert spirituality" because of the stark nothingness of the desert, this form of prayer seeks to rid an individual of all falsehood, attachments, and illusions in order to attend to God alone. Since God is transcendent, God is known in a kind of "unknowing." The well-known hymn describes "the hiddenness" of God that nurtures these practices.

> Holy, holy, holy!
> Though the darkness hide thee,
> though the eye of sinful man
> thy glory may not see,
> only thou art holy;
> there is none beside thee,
> perfect in power,
> in love and purity.[2]

Apophatic prayer is often seen as a "negative way" because it seeks to negate thoughts, feelings, and sensations other than a loving attentiveness to God. But we can also regard it as a way to open up very positive experiences. These practices do not diminish awareness of a real and personal God but heighten the inexpressible and ineffable nature of God. If in this form of contemplative prayer one can embrace an inward separation from the world, solitude, and silence—even briefly—one encounters and experiences the God who also dwells in separation, solitude, and silence. A truly holy communion takes place.

One of the oldest approaches to apophatic prayer comes from Eastern Orthodoxy. It is called "the Jesus prayer." The repetition of the prayer centers on the person and work of our Savior: "Lord Jesus Christ, Son of God, have mercy on me a sinner." It is a single phrase that can be spoken or thought often during the day and night. All other requests, concerns, or feelings are subjected to this one prayer until the prayer itself becomes a part of one's consciousness and subconsciousness. The prayer takes on a life of its own.[3]

Another approach in apophatic contemplation is Centering Prayer. In this practice, one chooses a sacred word as a way of giving permission to God's presence and action within. That word is used as an intentional consent to surrender to the indwelling Spirit and is repeated gently as often as necessary. The purpose of the word is to center one in the divine Presence when the mind is attracted to some thought or feeling.[4]

Contemplative prayer, in both its apophatic and kataphatic forms, is not just for academics or ascetics. One doesn't need to be a scholar or a monk to benefit from this way of praying. Nor is contemplative prayer a new practice. Rooted in scripture, it has been taught through the centuries and modeled by saints, some of whom are well-known and many whom are unknown. Contemplative prayer acts as a doorway through which we may continually walk to discover and discern the reality, presence, and love of the One in whom we live and move and have our being.

Reflection Questions

1. Recall any times when you have entered into contemplative prayer. Reflect on what motivated you and your experience of this way of praying. Describe your experience.

2. How have you experienced silence related to contemplative prayer? Has contemplative prayer led you into silence, or has silence been a requirement for contemplative prayer?

3. How can you experience the presence of Christ beyond mental or emotional experiences?

CHAPTER 5

Personal Transformation
Being Changed by the
Presence of Christ

Christ's presence compels and creates love, reorients and renews the human spirit toward compassion and kindness. That presence creates a whole new capacity to love God, neighbor, and self.

The greatest joys in life come from being loved and being able to love. We do not experience life's deepest meaning in activity, accumulation, or even in achievement but in love. Jesus summarized the Hebrew scriptures with two commands, "The first is . . . 'love the Lord your God with all your heart, and with all your soul, and with all your mind, and with all your strength.' The second is this, 'You shall love your neighbor as yourself'" (Mark 12:30-31). On another occasion Jesus said, "This is my commandment, that you love one another as I have loved you" (John 15:12).

Is it possible to learn how to love, really love? Is the kind of life that Jesus exemplified a real-life option for today? How does the presence of Christ change us? Can we be transformed into human beings that receive love, give love, and live in love?

It is at this very point that all of us struggle and fail. We want to love as Jesus commanded and we want to love as Jesus loved, but we find it incredibly difficult and often impossible. We pray and strive, yet our lives remain terribly chaotic and our behavior more selfish than we would like to admit.

Anger and anxiety characterize our lives more than patience and peace. We act in compulsive, competitive, and controlling ways. We have our addictions, though some of us hide them better than others. We lose our temper, and our tongues rattle off with meaningless chatter or hurtful diatribes. Then all of this produces grief and guilt because we don't want to live this way. A conflict rages inside us. We know we ought to love, and at times we desire it deeply; but still, more often than not, we do not do it.

Hear this good news: the experience of Christ's presence is transformative. That presence compels and creates love, reorients and renews the human spirit toward compassion and kindness. That presence creates a whole new capacity to love God, neighbor, and self. I remember the story of the woman who stood in a worship service to testify, "I'm not what I ought to be. I'm not what I'm going to be. But thank God, I'm not what I used to be."

Personal transformation is not left to us alone. We are not abandoned to our own will and wit. It is not just the warring elements in our personality that can determine the development of our character. A divine dimension beyond our psychic and emotional energy can empower us to love. An incredible gift is offered to us. Not only consolation, comfort, and companionship but Christ's real presence collaborates with us in the process of inward transformation. But exactly how does this transformation happen?

Transformation Takes Place in the Soul

The difficulty of personal, inward change causes some people to feel cynical and pessimistic about ever accomplishing it. Countless times I've heard someone say, "People don't change" or "You really can't change a person. You can change behavior, but you don't change his or her heart." Certainly anyone who has seriously sought personal transformation will readily testify to the challenge.

Changing long-held prejudices, deep-seated resentments, or paralyzing fears is not easy. The sicknesses of the soul may seem incurable. Maladies of the self are destructive and deadly and anything but easy to overcome. Because the biggest changes needed reside in the deepest recesses of the self, the real presence of Christ becomes critical. Indeed, this is the very place where the reality and power of Christ's presence make the greatest difference.

Receiving the presence of Christ and practicing the presence of Christ are inward realities, internal experiences. Christ's presence can and does alter the way we think and affects the way we feel. Christ's presence can and does strengthen the will, awaken the conscience, enlighten the imagination. Christ's presence can and does create motivation, inhibit destructive tendencies, and purify motives. And this transformation occurs in a way that is totally noncoercive and coherent with our identity and distinct individuality.

The influence comes through the intimacy and imminence of the presence of Christ. Christ is not outside us, working on us from a distance, whispering instructions from heaven. Rather, Christ is *within* us—calling, creating, and communing. Christ's presence is closer than the breath we breathe, nearer than the beat of our heart. Thomas Merton explains it in a profound way:

> The real point of the contemplative life has always been a deepening of faith and of the personal dimensions of liberty and apprehension to the point where our direct union with God is realized and "experienced." We awaken not only to a realization of the

immensity and majesty of God "out there" as King and Ruler of the universe (which his is) but also a more intimate and more wonderful perception of Him as directly and personally present in our own being. Yet this is not a pantheistic merger or confusion of our being with his. On the contrary, there is a distinct conflict in the realization that though in some sense He is more truly ourselves than we are, yet we are not identical with Him, and though He loves us better than we can love ourselves we are opposed to Him, and in opposing Him we oppose our own deepest selves. If we are involved only in our surface existence, in externals, and in the trivial concerns of our ego, we are untrue to Him and to ourselves. To reach a true awareness of Him as well as ourselves, we have to renounce our selfish and limited self and enter into a whole new kind of existence, discovering an inner center of motivation and love which makes us see ourselves and everything else in an entirely new light. Call it faith, call it (at a more advanced stage) contemplative illumination, call it the sense of God or even mystical union: all these are different aspects and levels of the same kind of realization: the awakening to a new awareness of ourselves in Christ, created in Him, redeemed by Him, to be transformed and glorified in and with Him.[1]

What a beautiful possibility the presence of Christ opens to us. What an awesome and amazing potential is offered. What a life-changing process is made available. We enter into a kind of dance with the divine, a living experiment; some of us would call it a relationship. Call it whatever you will, Christ's presence within us makes us into human beings with new capacity to receive and give love.

During this process, should we make specific requests? Should we ask that the presence of Christ work in a particular way? The answer is yes, but let us remember that we are asking, not demanding or bargaining. We can ask as a child would ask a parent for something.

I am a parent, and I know how much I love my children. When they were young and came to me with an honest and genuine request, I granted it if I could. But sometimes what they asked was not good for them or not the best for them. Because I loved them, I would not grant their request. So it is with God, whose wisdom and perfect understanding far exceeds our own. At times God as the perfect, loving parent cannot and will not grant our request, even if we think it's a good one.

But with all my heart I believe that if God can grant our request, God will. Why? Because God's love for us is infinite and God's desire is for our good. Especially, God desires our transformation. So, yes let us make requests, but let us trust the hidden yet real Presence. The infinite love indwelling us is more than sufficient and strong for what we need, whether we understand how that presence works or not. Again, Merton is helpful:

> This inner awareness, this experience of love as an immediate and dynamic presence, tends to alter our perspective. We see the prayer of petition a little differently. Celebration and praise, loving attention to the presence of God, become more important than "asking for" and "getting" things. We realize that in Him and with Him all good is present to us and to humankind: if we seek first the kingdom of Heaven, all the rest comes along with it. Hence we worry a great deal less about the details of our daily needs, and we trust God to take care of our problems even if we do not ask insistently at every minute to do so.[2]

Since the ways of the inner self are complex and subtle, we should not be shocked when change occurs in serendipities and surprises. In unexpected and unanticipated ways, we discover twists and turns within ourselves. We change, and at the time of change we ourselves are amazed. Only in retrospect can we see more clearly how and why certain shifts occurred.

Transformation Takes Place in Our Story

The presence of Christ works in our unfolding lives, in the everyday events, ordinary relationships, and simple choices we make. Everyday life is the place where transformation takes place because that is the location of divine presence and providence. Though it may not seem dramatic, living our life in the time and place we are given presents the opportunity to experience the transforming presence of Christ.

Transformation takes place as we get in touch with our story, listen to it, and learn from it. If we become attentive, the Spirit will open our eyes to see how God is already at work in our story. We will develop ears to hear what the Spirit would say to us about the uniqueness of our life's drama. We will nurture a heart to receive what God is trying to do in and for us. If we can have the discernment an amazing thing happens. We can actually begin to embrace our story as our own. We can even celebrate it. Our story actually becomes a song and this creates a greater space for the presence of Christ to make transformation.

For this to happen, we need to reflect on our past, even the bad parts of our past. I don't believe God causes bad things to happen to people. I do believe God can take even the bad and bring good out of it. Some of the bad in our past was caused by us; some was caused by others; and some was caused by the fact that we live in a fallen world. But whatever the cause, we can ask a gracious God to bring good out of it. God brings beauty out of ashes, joy out of mourning, order out of chaos. Of course, we may want just to forget parts of our past, but even such forgetfulness needs to be intentional rather than denial. We gain nothing by suppressing our past or hiding from it. By naming our past, we can own our story and move on to celebration.

Our story encompasses the present too, and it is the present we must treasure as a sacred trust. Each day is a gift to be enjoyed.

Each moment is to be relished. Indeed we can nurture the vocabulary of joy by affirming life and expressing thanks. This is not an appeal for a Pollyanna attitude or a pep talk on positive thinking but an encouragement to simple and profound gratitude for life. Dietrich Bonhoeffer offers insightful words about gratitude:

> In the Christian community thankfulness is just what it is anywhere else in the Christian life. Only he who gives thanks for little things receives the big things. We prevent God from giving us the great spiritual gifts his has in store for us, because we do not give thanks for daily gifts. We think we dare not be satisfied with the small measure of spiritual knowledge, experience, and love that has been given to us, and that we must constantly be looking forward eagerly for the highest good. Then we deplore the fact that we lack the deep certainty, the strong faith, and the rich experience that God has given to others, and we consider this lament to be pious. We pray for the big things and forget to give thanks for the ordinary, small (and yet really not small) gifts. How can God entrust great things to one who will not thankfully receive from Him the little things? If we do not give thanks daily for the Christian fellowship in which we have been placed, even where there is no great experience, no discoverable riches, but much weakness, small faith, and difficulty; if on the contrary, we only keep complaining to God that everything is so paltry and petty, so far from what we expected, then we hinder God from letting our fellowship grow according to the measure and riches which are there for us all in Jesus Christ.[3]

Faith in Christ does not shield us from pain and problems, difficulties and disappointments. The present often is a strange mixture of pain and pleasure. Successes and failures can occur simultaneously. Joy and sorrow are often concurrent. The present can bring on the desire to laugh and cry in the same moment. Yet it is this present that we treasure and cherish. Perhaps it is not the one we expected or one we would have chosen for ourselves, yet it is our story. And whether we feel it or not, the presence of Christ is in the middle of it. So let us celebrate it.

In a further step of faith, let us anticipate the future. My favorite story about the future is one I heard from a Native American in Kansas City, Missouri, several years ago. It seems that as the winter was approaching, all the Indians went to the chief and asked, "What kind of winter will we have?" to which he responded, "It's going to be a very hard winter." Because of this pronouncement, they all went out to gather firewood. The chief, a little worried, called the weather bureau and asked the same question. They answered, "It will be a hard winter." The chief felt better and returned to his accustomed place only to have the tribe ask him again, "Are you sure we're going to have a difficult winter?" He answered, "Yes." And they went to gather more firewood. The chief was now very worried so he called the weather bureau a second time and asked the same question, "Are you sure we're going to have a difficult winter?" And they answered the same way, "Yes." This time the chief asked the weather bureau, "How do you know we're going to have a difficult winter?" And they answered, "Because the Indians are gathering firewood."

The moral of this story is that no one really knows the future. Even though some people make a lot of money trying to predict it, and though there are futurists in both business and religion, no one can see into tomorrow. But the One who is at work in our past and present will be at work in our future. The future shines as brightly as the presence and promise of God. And these are as true as the goodness and greatness of God.

> Great is thy faithfulness,
> O God my Father;
> there is no shadow of turning with Thee;
> thou changest not, thy compassions they fail not;
> as thou hast been, thou forever wilt be.[4]

We can anticipate our future. However, in that anticipation let me say that the future is also as bright as the choices we make and the faith we exhibit. I do not believe the future is already fixed or determined. The future chapters in our story are not already written. Rather, we participate in shaping our future. Our decisions and our actions have real consequences and real results. And so our story unfolds as we cooperate with God in trust and obedience.

Transformation takes place in the real story of our life. So let us remember and reflect on our past and learn from it. Let us treasure our present and enjoy it. Let us anticipate our future and work toward it. We need not give in to cynicism or despair. We need not worry and fret about what could have been or what might be. We need not be afraid of the darkness around us or the difficulties ahead of us. For transformation to take place, we should believe God and do our best. We should love God and be amazed at what will happen. We should wait on God and watch God do wonderful things in our story.

Transformation Takes Place in Our Struggles

Anyone who says that personal, moral, spiritual transformation will be easy is not telling the truth. People who promise quick results and simple solutions to complex problems and long-term issues either unwittingly or intentionally deceive others. The grace of our Lord Jesus Christ is free and abundant, but it is not cheap. Because divine grace and human effort are not mutually exclusive in this lifelong quest for transformation, all respected guides in the life of faith speak of "practicing the disciplines," "fighting the good fight," or "subduing the passions." Transformation involves struggle, and actually it is in the struggle itself that we experience transformation.

Scripture speaks of struggling with the world, the flesh, and the devil, and working out our salvation (see Phil. 2:12). The "world" does not mean the created cosmos of beauty and order but the systems and structures of human society that compete for our allegiance and loyalty. This systemic, all-pervasive environment founded on greed, pride, and lust can overpower and deform human beings, destroy virtue, and defeat noble efforts to provide for the common good. The apostle Paul tells us, "Do not be conformed to this world" (Rom. 12:2). And John says, "Do not love the world" (1 John 2:15-16). Jesus himself told his disciples, "If the world hates you, keep in mind that it hated me first" (John 15:18, NIV).

I grew up in a church culture where "worldliness" was defined in what now seem silly terms. For instance, I was taught that a Christian shouldn't go to movies or watch TV. Various sectarian organizations promote nonconformity to the world in terms of dress or forbid participation in public society. There has always been a tendency in Christian circles to withdraw from the world or be isolated from the world as a way of following Christ. Today it is easier to laugh at or scorn others' trivial and bizarre rules rather than to take seriously our own struggle with the world.

Don't underestimate the seriousness or subtlety around us that we are called to resist. In a competitive culture, sports can be a false religion. Billions of dollars promote sports and build the temples where people "worship" in frenzy with the mantra "winning is everything." In a consumer and materialistic culture, free enterprise can be a false religion. The god of this religion is the bottom line; its mantra is "the one who has the most things wins." In a sensate culture, entertainment can be a false religion whose god is the body. Sexual pleasure and satisfaction become its holy grail. In a violent culture, military power can be a false religion with the mantra "might makes right." Its prophets and priests are more often politicians than generals. In a secular culture, scientism can be a false religion. Its places of worship are academic centers where their evangelists proclaim that the origin and meaning of life can be understood in human terms alone.

These and other expressions of the world harbor disdain for Christ. And well they should! The ethic of Christ is a threat to and a judgment of the world. The way of Christ condemns each of these ways of culture and creates a counterculture. Christ prays not that we would be taken out of the world but that we would be protected from the world (see John 17:11). We are to live as aliens and strangers in this world, refusing to live by its standards, values, and priorities. This is a struggle, but in this struggle comes our transformation.

We are also called to struggle with our flesh, which is a biblical way to describe the sinful part of our human nature. I like Parker Palmer's reference to the "shadow self."[5] Others have called it our "false self." "The flesh" describes that capacity and tendency we have to act selfishly, foolishly, and unlovingly. No one needs to convince me of the reality of this inward conflict between what I know is right and what is wrong. My greatest problem is not confusion but division. I know myself to be divided internally. To use the words of scripture, "I do not understand my own actions. For I do not do what I want, but I do the very thing I hate. . . . Now if I do what I do not want, it is no longer I that do it, but sin that dwells within me" (Rom. 7:15, 20).

I can offer two words of encouragement for this struggle with the flesh that leads to transformation. First, let it be clear that the root of this struggle is not in our physical bodies. Some have mistakenly hated their bodies and abused them under the illusion that the body is bad while the spirit is good. Physical appetites, including the sexual appetite, are not evil in themselves. God created our bodies as good, and the biblical reference to "the flesh" does not refer to the physical. Although ascetic practices have a long history in the church and may be useful for some, we will struggle under false pretenses if we think our tendencies to sin are somehow rooted in our embodied nature.

Second, I encourage simple fortitude and perseverance. I am inspired by the lives of many who have gone before us. Countless Christians have lived in far more difficult circumstances than I can imagine. They have faced much greater challenges or carried much greater responsibilities. Yet they demonstrated self-control and self-denial.

We struggle not only with the world and the flesh but also with

3.

the devil and a host of demonic spirits. It is a cosmic struggle. That may sound strange to modern and postmodern ears, but even Jesus spoke of an evil greater than collective human evil. There are powers that are not flesh and blood. There are "principalities and powers" at work in the world, an evil that defies description manifested throughout history. When people encounter it, they intuitively and instinctively call it demonic, even if they do not believe in a personal devil. This kind of evil is inexplicable. The gulags, concentration camps, killings fields, and genocides of history testify to its reality. If there isn't a personal devil with a legion of demons, we would have to invent one to help us cope. In his whimsical yet serious book *The Screwtape Letters* C. S. Lewis has probably helped more people than any other intellectual comprehend the possibility of a personalized evil operating in the world. That evil surely is not the caricature presented in today's horror movies, the "bogeyman" of occult practices, or the object of scorn attacked by televangelists in deliverance services. It is far more serious than any of that.

We can observe the demonic with which we struggle in the systemic evil of institutions, corporations, and governments that destroy people. We see it manifested in entrenched racism and horrendous prejudice. Institutions and organization that promote violence, pornography, or addiction provide more evidence of the demonic. It is seen in structures that perpetuate injustice and inequality and allow people who profess belief in God and goodness to participate in activities that demean human beings. Consider the historical institutions of slavery, apartheid, organized crime, and oppression. What else can you call these but demonic? And then there is war—senseless, mindless, brutality perpetuated in the name of national security or self-interest or even God.

We ignore or deny such evil at our own peril. We must take evil seriously so that we can resist it, shun it, and stand against it. We will do well to name such evil for what it is and where it comes from. It is ugly and it is demonic. Such naming need not create fear on our part but courage and conviction. We have an ally greater than our adversary: "The one who is in you is greater than the one who is in the world" (1 John 4:4). So we need not be afraid, and recognizing that is part of our transformation.

Transformation Takes Place in Our Suffering

Several years ago I heard Elisabeth Elliot describe suffering as anything to which you respond, "Oh, no." It can be as minor as a flat tire or a broken appliance that causes you to quickly say, "Oh, no." Or it can be the devastating news of a loved one's death that causes you to break down and weep, "Oh, my God, no." Pain is a part of life, and it seems we live our lives on a continuum of hurts, sometimes seen by others but more often unobserved.

On this continuum of pain, there are those simple incidents that interrupt our routine and cause inconvenience. Then there are those annoyances that irritate or agitate us. Then there are the stresses that cause real frustration or anxiety. And if the stress becomes intense enough, it turns to distress that can cause us to lose our balance. If the distress lasts long enough, it can be paralyzing. Then there is chronic sickness, a continuous disappointment or dysfunction that won't go away. Add to this continuum the hurt caused by betrayal, incurable disease, injustices in our family or society, natural disasters, violence, and war. And then, of course, there is death. There is a lot in life to which we respond, "Oh, no."

What shall we do with our pain? This to me is one of the acid tests of faith. How we handle our suffering and hurts will determine to a great degree how we handle the pain of the world. How we handle our own pain also will largely determine our own transformation. Will we deny our pain either in our attempt to "be happy" or because we can't explain it? Will we anesthetize ourselves to it, always look for a way out of it, or do everything we can to avoid facing and feeling it? Will we play the "blame game" or become angry or bitter? How we answer these questions will shape how suffering affects us.

I would like to suggest how the presence of Christ can work in our suffering to transform us. Pain is not so much a problem to be solved as it is a mystery to be embraced and endured. This is true because God is at work in our pain as well as in our pleasure. This is not to say that God causes our pain but that God loves us as much in our pain as in the rest of our lives. God promises us comfort and consolation in times of suffering. God promises strength to help us bear our hurts. God promises us wisdom to help us learn from our pain. God promises us grace to transform us through our pain and actually use it as an instrument of the transformation. So let us embrace pain, not as a friend but as a reality of life we cannot avoid. Let us allow pain to do its work in us, and let us trust the presence of Christ not as a way out but as a way in and through the pain.

Christ himself faced pain this way in his life and ministry. He refused to run, hide, or try to force his own agenda to avoid suffering. He faced it, accepted it, and endured it, trusting in the love of his Father. It was not easy. Suffering never is. That's why it is called suffering. And it can never be fully explained. That's why it is called mystery.

Suffering, whatever its source, can actually be used by the love and grace of God for our transformation and the transformation of others. For me this reality is the bedrock of faith. It is the foundation upon which we can build our lives. Nothing, and I do mean nothing, can separate us from the love of God. Pain is real, but God's love is equally real and is greater than our pain. This assurance brings transformation.

Reflection Questions

1. Reflect on the passage "We need to reflect on our past, even the bad parts of our past. I don't believe God causes bad things to happen to people. I do believe God can take even the bad and bring good out of it." When has this proved true in your life? Consider how any such experiences changed you.

2. "Pain is not so much a problem to be solved as it is a mystery to be embraced and endured. God is at work in our pain as well as in our pleasure." How do you respond to these statements? How does this perspective affirm or challenge your own?

3. If transformation is the result of cooperating with God, what does God do and what do we do? Think about any experiences of your own or that you have observed that illustrate this cooperation.

4. Can you discern and describe ways you have changed or experienced transformation? How did it happen?

CHAPTER 6

Christian Community

Experiencing the Presence of Christ with Others

In community all the different hues and colors of Christ are reflected and imaged. Nothing is quite so remarkable and amazing as Christian community. Nothing is quite so profound and powerful a witness to the world as Christian community.

What should the body of Christ look like? Answers vary depending on a person's perspective and presuppositions. From the perspective of social justice, the life of Jesus is a prophetic challenge to the status quo that calls for a simple lifestyle of self-denial and sacrifice. The evangelical perspective holds up Jesus as Savior, so the church's identity lies in proclaiming the crucified and resurrected Lamb who reconciles us to God.

Liberation theology presents Jesus as the great emancipator. Therefore, Christ's presence continues in the struggle of the poor, the oppressed, and the powerless. Feminist theology sees Jesus as not only liberator but unifier, bringing together male and female and all the disparate elements of the cosmos.

Charismatics envision Jesus as the one whose mighty works of healing, exorcisms, and miracles should characterize the body of Christ today along with an abiding sense of the Spirit. Sacramentalists experience the presence of Christ not only in the Eucharist but in eucharistic acts of mercy as well as the ordinary events of everyday life. Contemplatives view Jesus as a person of prayer; therefore, in their vision of the church, solitude, silence, and prayer are vital.

Is it any wonder that confusion abounds, not to speak of division and competition about the role of the church? What seems to be a noble vision or a simple desire quickly becomes a more challenging and daunting quest.

To be the presence of Christ is not quite as straightforward or as easy as we might think, because Christ himself is not quite as easy to understand as we have thought. Perhaps this Jesus of history, this Christ of faith is far more beautiful, far more radical, and far more profound than we have imagined.

Yet what seems hopelessly confusing about our different interpretations of Christ could actually demonstrate where experiencing the presence of Christ has its greatest impact—in community. No one of us can fully exhaust or interpret the living Christ alone. We need community. All the interpretations of Christ are not unlike the different hues of a diamond when held to the light. As it is rotated, the diamond's beauty and wonder are only magnified. In a similar fashion, the longer we look at Christ the more we sees his richness. And the differing perspectives only intensify that richness.

In community all the different hues and colors of Christ are reflected and imaged. Nothing is quite so remarkable and amazing as Christian community. Nothing is quite so profound and powerful a witness to the world as Christian community. In Christian community we have a place to affirm one another's perspectives and gifts and also recognize that none of us is the body of Christ by ourselves. No one of us can stand alone. No one of us has a corner on the truth. No one of us has a complete understanding of the gospel. We will be the presence of Christ by participating in community.

This is not an option. Being part of a community is essential for the kingdom of God to come on earth as it is in heaven, and it is also essential to personal fulfillment. For me, the richest experiences of life have not occurred in private moments of spiritual ecstasy. They have not occurred in intellectual quest or academic achievement but in the experience of community.

Historical Community

I'm sometimes amazed at the lack of historical perspective among Christians. It is as if only the present matters; events and expressions of today are unrelated to yesterday. For some, this disconnect with the past comes from ignorance. More disturbing is the realization that for others this disconnect is intentional. Some people disregard and even disdain history or tradition, adopting an attitude of superiority about present understandings and interpretations.

The writer of Hebrews admonishes faith and faithfulness with the symbol of a marathon runner surrounded by a cheering and encouraging audience (see Heb. 12:1). We who live in this world seeking to be the embodiment of Christ need to remember that there are a great host of followers who have gone on before us. Their successes and struggles not only inform us but inspire us. We can and should listen to their witness and learn from them.

Jaroslav Pelikan in his book *Jesus Through the Centuries* describes a series of images portraying Christ from the first century to the twenty-first century. He shows how the character of Christ has been understood in the historical culture and context of each age. In successive generations Jesus has been regarded as

> The Rabbi
> The Turning Point of History
> The Light of the Gentiles

The King of Kings
The Cosmic Christ
The Son of Man
The True Image
Christ Crucified
The Monk Who Rules the World
The Bridegroom of the Soul
The Divine and Human Model
The Universal Man
The Mirror of the Eternal
The Prince of Peace
The Teacher of Common Sense
The Poet of the Spirit
The Liberator
The Man Who Belongs to the World[1]

This brief historical enumeration illustrates the breadth of the body of Christ through the centuries. Christ has been understood, interpreted, and followed in many ways; and we would do well to learn from these earlier generations. We will not only be humbled and challenged, but we will be enriched and encouraged as we live within this historical community.

A significant principle is at stake here. When we define everything according to its relevance today, we imply that "today" has no touchstone or commonality with yesterday. The present is defined as "post-everything"—post-Christendom, postmodern, postdenominational—terms that open a great divide between "post" and all that has gone before. Such reasoning is foolish and absurd. We can no more separate ourselves from the past than we can separate ourselves from the future. And why would we want to? Church history definitely contains its dark chapters and great cruelties. But it also holds martyrs and mystics, poets and philosophers, and a host of unnamed saints who thought beautiful thoughts, performed heroic deeds, endured incredible circumstances, and through it all exemplified the character and compassion of Christ.

This historical church is our community. Let us celebrate it and participate in it. We can study the lives of biblical characters. We can learn the liturgical calendar and observe it. We can read and pray the prayers of those who have gone before us. We can meditate on the life of a saint before an icon or image. We can learn about the expansion of the gospel and the heroes of missions. We can visit a church with a tradition different from our own. We can form a friendship with a Christian believer with whom we have theological differences. But most important of all, we can and should see ourselves as inheritors and participants of a community that reaches back in time.

In fact, this community stretches beyond time. The cloud of witnesses that surrounds us includes those who are in the nearer presence of Christ. They have lived on earth in the past and now they live in glory. But they, along with us, are part of the same community. Hebrews 12:22-24 describes this community:

> You have come to Mount Zion and to the city of the living God, the heavenly Jerusalem, and to innumerable angels in festal gathering, and to the assembly of the firstborn who are enrolled in heaven, and to God the judge of all, and to the spirits of the righteous made perfect, and to Jesus, the mediator of a new covenant.

Here we have a symbolic yet real picture of a beautiful continuity and succession. We keep company with a great host of men and women who have loved and followed Christ. What a source of hope and encouragement, especially when we feel lonely or isolated. We not only inherit the collective wisdom of this historical community, but we can enjoy the unseen company of those who now inhabit eternity. We can experience community.

Global Community

The Christian community is not only ancient; it is global. How rich and beautiful is the worldwide body of Christ! Beginning with a ragtag group of disciples, the Christian movement has expanded to encircle the globe. And this should not surprise us because the goal of the gospel is that "the kingdom of the world has become the kingdom of our Lord and of his Messiah" (Rev. 11:15). One of the most beautiful hymns of praise to Christ celebrates the end of history:

> You are worthy to take the scroll
>   and to open its seals,
> for you were slaughtered and by
>   your blood you ransomed
>   for God
>   saints from every tribe and language
>   and people and nation;
> you have made them to be a
>   kingdom and priests
>   serving our God,
> and they shall reign upon the earth.—Revelation 5:9-10

We do not need to wait until the end of history to see this grand picture of community created from all nationalities and ethnicities. Already, if we have eyes to see, the diversity of the Christian community staggers us. It is multicultural, multilingual, and still growing. Perhaps the twentieth century witnessed as great an expansion of the church as any century in history, and this ancient faith continues to find fresh expressions around the world. Words like *adaptation*, *indigenous*, *contextual* help explain why this global community continues to grow and why it is both unchanging and ever changing at the same time.

The day of colonial missions is over. The day when Western culture and Western denominations imposed their culture on other parts of the body of Christ is over. But the day when Christians from all over the world in mutual trust and respect can work together, pray together, and learn from one another is just beginning. We live as part of a global Christian community in which we have the opportunity to engage in collaborative mission.

We can exchange ideas and information with relative ease. We can dialogue, discuss, and even debate theological differences (as well as find similarities), enriching our understanding of the faith. We can partner across geographical, theological, and national boundaries for shared ministry. We can transcend secular political differences because we are brothers and sisters in Christ. But most of all, we can experience a global community and participate in it.

Again I must confess that the lack of global perspective among so many followers of Christ in North America surprises me. The narrowness and provincialism among some is mind boggling. Do we want to capture Christ for our own culture alone and make him in our own image? Do we want all followers of Christ to conform to our culture or to ignore other cultures, living as if we alone know and love Christ? This ethnocentric phenomenon probably exists all over the world, but I believe North American Christians are particularly prone to it. We have grown a consumer church whose primary purpose is to deliver religious goods and services that cater to the felt needs of its members and its potential members. Consequently our focus and attention seldom become global. Another reason we're slow to embrace global community might be fear of cultures so different from what we know.

Vincent Donovan's book *Christianity Rediscovered: An Epistle from the Masai* includes the following creed. Notice the cultural nuances from an African tribal people. Let it be one example, among many thousands, of how the experience of global community can enrich us.

> We believe in the one High God, who out of love created the beautiful world and everything good in it. He created man and wanted man to be happy in the world. God loves the world and every nation and tribe on the earth. We have known this High God in the darkness, and now we know him in the light. God promised in the book of his word, the Bible, that he would save the world and all the nations and tribes.

We believe that God made good his promise by sending his son, Jesus Christ, a man in the flesh, a Jew by tribe, born poor in a little village, who left his home and was always on safari doing good, curing people by the power of God, teaching about God and man, showing that the meaning of religion is love. He was rejected by his people, tortured and nailed hands and feet to a cross and died. He lay buried in the grave, but the hyenas did not touch him, and on the third day, he rose from the grave. He ascended to the skies. He is the Lord.

We believe that all our sins are forgiven through him. All who have faith in him must be sorry for their sins, be baptized in the Holy Spirit of God, live the rules of love and share the bread together in love, to announce the good news to others until Jesus comes again. We are waiting for him. He is alive. He lives. This we believe. Amen.[2]

Local Community

As great as the witness of an individual saint may be, we see even greater witness in saints living, loving, praying, and serving in community. Simply stated, nothing in the world is more beautiful than the body of Christ functioning in a local context.

We actually have most difficulty experiencing community at the local level. Local-church community challenges all our prejudices and power-hungry tendencies. It requires the most grace because it requires the most intimacy and involvement with others. Making ourselves known in close community is risky. We must become vulnerable in ways that differ from the work environment. Yet if we choose to take the risk, we can discover more about ourselves. Living in authentic local community is one of the most challenging and demanding commands of Christ to obey. And yet it is what the world needs and wants from Christians more than anything else.

When the world sees genuine Christian community at a local level, it sees the very presence of Christ.

Jesus' radical concept of community generated controversy in his own time. He practiced and created community. He ate with sinners and identified with outcasts. He didn't see a hierarchical relationship between men and women but treated them as equals. He was unimpressed with status and the artificial divisions between people. For Christ, people were more important than institutions or traditions. And he had great compassion and love.

In a similar fashion, for us, participating in community means nurturing relationships and making peace. It means building bridges and breaking down barriers between people. Whenever and wherever possible, we nurture understanding. We become peacemakers who do not live in isolation and retreat from one another. Rather we live in loving, vulnerable relationships.

Christian community can and does happen in a variety of settings—prayer cells, accountability groups, occasional gatherings—but the greatest expression of local community takes place in the local congregation where the Word is proclaimed, the supper is celebrated, believers are baptized, married, and buried. There is no substitute for the church, not only the historical, global, and triumphant church but the local reality.

Missional Community

Christian community in all its expressions—historical, global, and local—differs from other forms of community because it is created by Christ to extend his redemptive mission in the world. It surely bears similarities to other kinds of human communities—towns, fraternities, societies, associations, and so forth. But since it exists to partake of and participate in God's reconciling mission to the world in Jesus Christ, the Christian community is unique.

Christian community is a means to an end. It is to represent, serve, and proclaim the kingdom of God. Its goal is not to build up an institution or to enlarge its membership or even to enjoy its own existence. Rather, the purpose of Christian community is faithfulness to God's mission in the world. Its very identity and essence define it as a missional community.

To experience Christian community, we must first discern God's great mission to restore and heal a broken creation through Jesus Christ; then we discover how to participate in that mission. Enjoying the company of other Christians, being nice and polite to other Christians, and attending meetings with other Christians do not equate with Christian community. Christian community means more than being a member of a support group, recovery group, self-help group, or therapy group. And it is more than consuming the personal, social, and cultural benefits offered in a corporation-like organization.

To experience the community that Christ creates, we must be captured by the vision of Christ's mission and be consumed by a passion for that mission. Nothing will draw people together in unity and joy like a vision and passion for God's reconciling mission in Jesus Christ. Nothing will break down the walls of separation, destroy prejudices among us, and heal the hurts among us like a shared vision and passion for God's mission in the world.

Reflection Questions

1. How does Christian community differ from community in any other context?

2. Why is it so difficult for us to practice community as followers of Christ?

3. Where have you experienced authentic Christian community that has been transformative for you and others?

CHAPTER 7

Pain and Sacrifice

Embracing the Presence of Christ in Suffering

Self-sacrifice is necessary in the way of Christ and in the
way of being the presence of Christ.

The Christian gospel claims that greatness comes through humility. Self-fulfillment comes through denial. Life comes through death. The Cross symbolizes paradox. The cross on which Christ died is not only an historical reality and the foundation for our faith as Christians, it is also the model by which we must live if we are to be the presence of Christ in the world. His invitation is clear: "If any want to become my followers, let them deny themselves and take up their cross and follow me" (Matt. 16:24).

Even more amazing, we are to find joy by embracing this paradox, by living sacrificially, by considering it a privilege. On the surface this concept may seem morbid or even masochistic. It sounds like Christ is calling us to enjoy suffering. Not so. Suffering is not to be enjoyed. It is to be endured. Christ himself shuddered before the cross, wept, and asked that he be spared the suffering. Anyone who reads the biblical accounts with imagination can readily see that the cross was a painful and shameful experience. Yet the night before his death, he told the disciples he wanted them to have the joy that he had (see John 15:11).

I believe Jesus was the most joy-filled person who ever lived, even though he was called "the Man of Sorrows." Here is one of the first lessons to learn: sacrifice and joy are not mutually exclusive. In fact, to live sacrificially—even though painful at times—is the most fulfilling and rewarding way to live.

Life is much more than existence, survival, and self-preservation. The human ego always demands more, always clamors for attention, always seeks gratification. It must be denied. The ego must be lost in a greater cause, a grander vision, a nobler purpose than itself. Self-sacrifice is necessary in the way of Christ and in the way of being the presence of Christ. But what does that mean?

How do we embrace the Cross of Christ not only as the sacrifice that atones for our sins but also as the pattern by which we live our lives? How do we exemplify before the world our faith in Christ, love for Christ, and obedience to Christ by following him through death into resurrection? How do we embrace sacrifice?

Offer Forgiveness

A good starting place is offering forgiveness to those who have injured us. The act and attitude of forgiveness may be as difficult and yet as Christlike as anything else in life. Alexander Pope said, "To err is human, to forgive divine." But we are called to forgive as humans because in Christ, God has forgiven us. And just as God's forgiveness of us preceded our repentance, so our forgiveness of others must precede their repentance. This always requires sacrifice.

Several years ago our home was robbed. The thieves took several items, including the piggy banks of our two preschool sons.

The loss was devastating to both of them. Several nights after the incident, I was putting the boys to bed and suggested that we pray for the robbers as Jesus taught us to pray for those who hurt us. After a long silence, my older son said, "Do you mean you want me to pray for the men who stole my piggy bank?" I answered yes and then asked the question, "Why do you think the robbers did what they did?" To which the second son replied, "I guess it's because they didn't love Jesus." The older son quickly answered, "Yes, and they are going to hell because of it." This prompted another question from the younger son who said, "Dad, will there be real fire in hell?" To which I responded, "Boys, let's get this conversation back on the main subject."

In their simple ways, both boys were doing what we all do when hurt or injured. We become angry and want revenge and judgment. Or we want to engage in all kinds of theological, philosophical, rhetorical debates, avoiding our personal responsibility to respond to injury like Christ.

At no place do I realize more how little I am like Christ than in the practice of forgiveness. Not only do I tend to hold a grudge, seek revenge, and become bitter toward someone who sins against me, but I can actually find pleasure in such feelings. Contrary to my better judgment, I can nurture my resentment and enjoy it in my imagination. I'm ashamed to admit these feelings and practices form part of my reality.

Sacrifice means denying this reality, refusing to let these feelings control me, rejecting these attitudes as unacceptable. Sacrifice means that when both my reason and emotions scream that it's understandable and justifiable to hate and return in kind what someone has done to me, I listen instead to the presence of Christ: Christ lovingly tells me to forgive.

Forgiveness contradicts the laws of nature and the laws of religion. In what some call "the real world," the rules are "an eye for an eye," "get even," "might makes right." The world regards forgiveness as a sign of weakness. In fact, it signifies a greater strength; it is the only act that can break the vicious cycle of sin and selfishness.

The offer of forgiveness does not guarantee redemption in the heart of the one to whom forgiveness is offered. The offer can be rejected. A relationship may not be restored by the practice of forgiveness, but forgiveness has within it the power to create a new reality, a changed relationship. The sacrifice of forgiveness holds the real possibility of transformation. This transformation takes place in the heart of the person who offers forgiveness whether or not it takes place in the heart of the one to whom forgiveness is offered.

So how do we as humans, so prone to anger and hatred, live such sacrifice and offer forgiveness? We look at Christ. Again and again, we hold before us the symbol of his sacrifice, which is the Cross. Even while he was dying Christ forgave. The writer of Hebrews says it this way,

> Looking to Jesus the pioneer and perfecter of our faith, who for the sake of the joy that was set before him endured the cross, disregarding its shame, and has taken his seat at the right hand of the throne of God. Consider him who endured such hostility against himself from sinners, so that you may not grow weary or lose heart.—Hebrews 12:2-3

Violence begets violence; anger begets anger; sin begets sin; but forgiveness begets reconciliation. To embrace sacrifice by the practice of forgiveness does not guarantee redemption, but without it, there can be no redemption.

Obedience When It's Not Easy

Sometimes the simplest, yet most difficult, way to be the presence of Christ is to do the right thing. No amount of religious ritual or pious rhetoric can substitute for being responsible, obeying the dictates of conscience or the commands of scripture. Doing the right thing requires effort, self-will, and discipline, all of which amount to a real form of sacrifice.

More so than public displays of spiritual devotion, God values faithfulness in the smallest duty—even when no person notices it. That fact actually creates one of our greatest problems, doesn't it? We tend to be "people pleasers" or religious exhibitionists more than devoted followers of Jesus Christ. We want others to applaud us or at least notice and recognize the good that we do. So we keep at least one eye on what others think or say about us. We get our feelings hurt if we are not congratulated for our good works; and if by chance our good works are misinterpreted or criticized, we are absolutely devastated.

How differently Christ acted during his earthly ministry. Singly focused on pleasing God and doing the will of God, he was not deterred from doing what was right by human custom or tradition. He didn't listen to the criticisms of religious leaders or the murmuring of the multitudes or even the misguided suggestions of his disciples. He listened only to his heavenly Father and obeyed the will of his heavenly Father. This kind of obedience cost him dearly. He faced ridicule, mockery, rejection, and ultimately crucifixion. Yet in this radical obedience Christ became our Savior.

For us to be obedient to the purposes and will of God is not easy. It also will cost us. At times obedience will require us to be kind to someone who doesn't "deserve" our kindness. Obedience means we relinquish the need to be right, to win, to be in control. Obedience may require us to give up our position or our prejudice. Obedience nearly always means letting go of ambition and putting others before ourselves. Obedience says no to the pride so deeply rooted within our human ego and says yes to the love and longing rooted even deeper in our spirit. All this is costly.

Consider the cost of obeying the teachings of Christ listed here:

> Love your enemies and pray for those who persecute you.—Matthew 5:44

> Do not worry about your life, what you will eat or what you will drink, or about your body what you will wear.—Matthew 6:25

Do not judge.—Matthew 7:1

Truly I tell you, whoever does not receive the kingdom of God as a little child will never enter it. —Mark 10:15

If anyone would come after me, he must deny himself and take up his cross and follow me.—Mark 8:34, NIV

Sell your possessions, and give alms. Make purses for yourselves that do not wear out, an unfailing treasure in heaven, where no thief comes near and no moth destroys.—Luke 12:33

No slave can serve two masters; for a slave will either hate the one and love the other, or be devoted to the one and despise the other. You cannot serve God and wealth.—Luke 16:13

I give you a new commandment, that you love one another. Just as I have loved you, you also should love one another.—John 13:34

If the world hates you, be aware that it hated me before it hated you. If you belonged to the world, the world would love you as its own. Because you do not belong to the world, but I have chosen you out of the world—therefore the world hates you. —John 15:18-19

To embrace sacrifice by the way of obedience does not mean that we are trying to save ourselves through our own efforts. Salvation is always God's gift of grace. We receive this grace by faith. But if our faith does not result in obedience, it is not authentic faith. So embracing sacrifice through obedience does not become performance-based religion, always trying to earn God's favor. Nor does obedience equate with righteousness attained by good works. Rather, our obedience is faith working in and through love.

When we value God's will above all else, we seek God's will above else. When we treasure God's purposes as expressions of God's love, we desire those purposes more than we desire our own selfish purposes. We, who have received the living presence of Christ and experienced the grace and beauty from that presence, can willingly embrace the sacrifice that obedience requires. Though it may be painful, we know it to be life-giving.

Why is obedience so difficult and often painful? I'm sure there are many answers to this question, but I confess that there is, for me, something of a mystery here. Christ himself is said to have "learned obedience through what he suffered," even though he was the Son of God (Heb. 5:8). Before his death, Christ agonized and even asked that he be allowed not to die. Yet he submitted to the cross as an act of obedience to the will of God. His famous prayer in the garden, "Not my will, but thine, be done" (Luke 22:42, KJV) perfectly articulates the relationship of obedience to sacrifice.

When we are confronted with a decision, we have the choice to do what's right or not to do it. We can obey, or we can refuse to obey. To obey is to embrace sacrifice.

Open Yourself to Human Suffering

For me the most sobering text in Holy Scripture is the picture Jesus paints of the last judgment as recorded in Matthew 25:31-46:

> When the Son of Man comes in his glory, and all the angels with him, then he will sit on the throne of his glory. All the nations will be gathered before him, and he will separate people one from another as a shepherd separates the sheep from the goats, and he will put the sheep at his right hand and the goats at the left. Then the king will say to those at his right hand, "Come, you that are blessed by my Father,

inherit the kingdom prepared for you from the foundation of the world; for I was hungry and you gave me food, I was thirsty and you gave me something to drink, I was a stranger and you welcomed me, I was naked and you gave me clothing, I was sick and you took care of me, I was in prison and you visited me." Then the righteous will answer him, "Lord, when was it that we saw you hungry and gave you food, or thirsty and gave you something to drink? And when was it that we saw you a stranger and welcomed you, or naked and gave you clothing? And when was it that we saw you sick or in prison and visited you?" And the king will answer them, "Truly I tell you, just as you did it to one of the least of these who are members of my family, you did it to me." Then he will say to those at his left hand, "You that are accursed, depart from me into the eternal fire prepared for the devil and his angels; for I was hungry and you gave me no food, I was thirsty and you gave me nothing to drink, I was a stranger and you did not welcome me, naked and you did not give me clothing, sick and in prison and you did not visit me." Then they also will answer, "Lord, when was it that we saw you hungry or thirsty or a stranger or naked or sick or in prison, and did not take care of you?" Then he will answer them, "Truly I tell you, just as you did not do it to one of the least of these, you did not do it to me." And these will go away into eternal punishment, but the righteous into eternal life.

This text teaches that a final human accountability before Christ, the King of the universe, will take place. A great divide exists between sheep and goats, righteous and unrighteous. And the criteria for judgment relate to how we have responded to human suffering. In fact, Christ identifies himself with those who suffer, saying our response to human suffering is the measure of our response to him.

This compelling and profound statement offered by our Lord confronts us with an ultimate question, *Will we open ourselves to those who suffer so that we see them, empathize with them, and, most importantly, act in compassion to help them?* If we do, it will cost us, because truly to help those who suffer requires time, tears, and treasure. We become vulnerable and available to them. We become involved personally, emotionally, and practically in their lives. We will have embraced sacrifice.

This text, however, not only addresses us as individuals; it also addresses churches as functioning congregations and the church as a corporate body. The future judgment that will be pronounced by Christ himself has more to do with our behavior and actions toward those who suffer than with our religious rituals or even our confessional statements. The real test of our faith is not what we sing or say we believe but what our belief has caused us to do, particularly for the suffering.

Jesus' explanation sounds very much like the Old Testament prophets who constantly rebuked Israel for substituting public and private worship for actions of justice and mercy to the suffering. Here's what Isaiah said in 1:11–17:

> What to me is the multitude of your sacrifices?
>   says the LORD;
> I have had enough of burnt offerings of rams
>   and the fat of fed beasts;
> I do not delight in the blood of bulls,
>   or of lambs, or of goats.
> When you come to appear before me,
>   who asked this from your hand?
>   Trample my courts no more;
> bringing offerings is futile;
>   incense is an abomination to me.

New moon and sabbath
   and calling of convocation—
   I cannot endure solemn assemblies with iniquity.
Your new moons and your appointed festivals
   my soul hates;
they have become a burden to me,
   I am weary of bearing them.
When you stretch out your hands,
   I will hide my eyes from you;
even though you make many prayers,
   I will not listen;
   your hands are full of blood.
Wash yourselves; make yourselves clean;
   remove the evil of your doings from before my eyes;
cease to do evil,
   learn to do good;
seek justice,
   rescue the oppressed,
defend the orphan,
   plead for the widow.

This ancient text has a similar ring to Jesus' words. People of faith are often blind to their own culpability and fail to see what is important to God. And just what is important to God? It ought to be obvious that what is important to God is a suffering humanity. God loves this broken world. God empathizes and sympathizes with poor and oppressed people. God knows every person and cares for every person.

Contrary to what we may feel or think at times, suffering does not signal God's absence in the world. Suffering does not mean God loves us less. Instead, God actually enters into suffering and shares it with us.

The world's pain is Christ's pain. He knows every tear that falls, and his heart still breaks over the human family for which he died. Christ hurts with and for every person in sickness and suffering.

Scripture puts it this way, "We have not a high priest which cannot be touched with the feeling of our infirmities" (Heb. 4:15, KJV). He is able to sympathize with us because he tasted the human condition. What a Savior!

And this Savior, whose wounds are yet visible, wants to live within us, so we can participate with him in caring for a suffering humanity. He wants to use our arms as his arms to put around an orphan child. He wants to use our hands as his hands to offer clean water to the thirsty. He wants to use our minds to find cures for diseases. He wants to use our imaginations as his to design a society that takes care of the powerless and protects the weak. He wants to use our resolve and determination as his to create and build a just society.

The standard for a Christian social ethic must ultimately be defined by the Cross of Christ. We simply cannot live in this world indifferent to its pain. Rather, like Christ, we must make the world's pain our own pain. We must experience a solidarity with those Jesus described as "the least of these." We must see ourselves in the tortured faces of those who experience loss.

The distinctions and differences that divide us are unimportant. Our quarrels and animosities are petty. Our cultural prejudices and racial rivalries are absurd. Even our personal, collective hostilities are insignificant. Why? Because we are related and connected to those who suffer by a common humanity. There is a basic unity within the human family. This kinship, which is more fundamental to our humanity than language, culture, or politics, compels us to sacrificial action.

Reflection Questions

1. "Self-sacrifice is necessary in the way of Christ and in the way of being the presence of Christ." If the way of Christ is the way of sacrifice, why do you think so many modern interpretations of the Christian faith ignore it?

2. What is the most difficult part of forgiving another person, and what makes it so?

3. How can we embrace the suffering of humanity without losing our joy?

CHAPTER 8

Engagement and Ministry

Being the Presence
of Christ as a Servant

*The ministry of Christ continues in and through us. What
he did while on earth we can do now. And with the power
of his indwelling Spirit, we can perform his works. In fact,
according to his promise, we can perform even greater
works because he is alive and active in us.*

On one occasion Jesus said that he came into the world not to be
served to serve (see Matt. 20:28). On another occasion, he told his
disciples that if they wanted to be great, they should seek to
become servants (see Mark 10:43). On the night before he died,
Jesus washed his disciples' feet, an act usually performed by house-
hold slaves. Clearly Jesus took upon himself the role of a servant
and expects us to do the same.

To be a continuing presence of Christ in the world calls us to
live our lives as servants of Christ ministering to one another and

to the world in his name. We will engage in ministry out of our gift-edness and in collaboration with others, but our very identity and self-understanding will be shaped by the actions, activities, and attitudes of a servant.

The ministry of Christ continues in and through us. What he did while on earth we can do now. And with the power of his indwelling spirit, we can perform his works. In fact, according to his promise, we can perform even greater works because he is alive and active in us (see John 14:12).

The ministry of Christ combined both proclamation and compassion for human need. He spoke truth that people needed to hear as a preacher and a teacher. Many listened to him with amazement because he taught with authority and clarity. Yet Jesus also cared for people's physical, emotional, and social problems. His miracles were, among other things, acts of mercy and kindness.

Christ commands us to make disciples of all nations (Matt. 28:19) and to love our neighbor as ourselves (Mark 12:31). Therefore, if we embody the presence of Christ in the world, we will engage in ministries of both word and deed.

Ministry of Word

We too are to speak Christ's words to both those who believe in him and those who do not. The truth that Christ taught is the truth we are to speak. It is a never-ending task, because there will always be those who do not know his truth or understand his truth.

For us to speak Christ's words, the truth conveyed in Christ's words must become truth to and for us. We ourselves must always be learners, students and disciples of his truth. Then we can speak his truth to others. We become witnesses and messengers for the truth that is in Christ.

I don't believe that we are responsible for converting people. Only the Holy Spirit can do that. We do, however, have the privilege and responsibility to tell our story and tell the Jesus story. Ours is the responsibility to speak boldly about God's love for all people.

Scripture records this command in many forms, but I love the one in 1 Peter 3:15-16: "but in your hearts sanctify Christ as Lord. Always be ready to make your defense to anyone who demands from you an accounting for the hope that is in you; yet do it with gentleness and reverence. Keep your conscience clear, so that, when you are maligned, those who abuse you for your good conduct in Christ may be put to shame."

For this ministry of the word, people may become evangelists, church planters, or missionaries going to difficult and dangerous places. Others become linguists and Bible translators. Still others become educators and teachers, scholars and researchers. And all of us can be witnesses. In winsome and welcome ways, each of us can engage in conversation about the truth that sets people free.

As a boy riding in the backseat of the family car I used to see a roadside sign: "Christ is the Answer." I didn't think too much of it until college when I heard a cynic ask, "Yes, but what's the question?" Over the passing years I have struggled, as have so many, with a number of philosophies and worldviews. As I grow older I become more and more convinced that indeed Christ is the Answer. Christ himself is the truth.

Christ is the answer to the question of life's origin, "For in him all things in heaven and on earth were created, things visible and invisible, whether thrones or dominions or rulers or powers—all things have been created through him and for him" (Col. 1:16).

Christ is the answer to the question of life's destiny, "For in him all the fullness of God was pleased to dwell, and through him God was pleased to reconcile to himself all things, whether on earth or in heaven, by making peace through the blood of his cross" (Col. 1:19-20).

Christ is the answer to the question of life's meaning, "The thief comes only to steal and kill and destroy. I came that they may have life, and have it abundantly" (John 10:10).

Christ is the answer to the question of life after death. Jesus said, "I am the resurrection and the life. Those who believe in me, even though they die, will live" (John 11:25).

So in a pluralistic world of competing voices and a marketplace of ideas, we proclaim Jesus Christ. Why? Because Jesus presents himself to us not only as God's representative or God's servant but as one whose relationship to God, origin from God, oneness with God, and life in God make him unlike any other human being who has ever lived. Jesus presents himself to us as the one who by his death on the cross is the world's Savior. He offers himself as the one who, because of his obedience to God in death, reconciles us to God. Jesus presents himself as the one who overcomes death. He is resurrected after his crucifixion and offers his eternal and abiding presence to all who will receive it.

So we unapologetically proclaim Christ to all. For those who will respond in faith and obedience we unapologetically teach Christ. The continuing teaching ministry of the church is central to its mission. For this ministry of the Word, some are pastors and teachers; others are professors and researchers. All of us can be students and learners of the Word, who can engage in conversations about the truth that has set us free.

Ministry of Deeds

The ministry of Christ encompasses not only words but also deeds. When John the Baptist inquired whether Jesus was indeed the Christ, the answer pointed to what could be seen as well as what was heard. Jesus said, "Go and tell John what you hear and see: the blind receive their sight, the lame walk, the lepers are cleansed, the deaf hear, the dead are raised and the poor have good news brought to them" (Matt. 11: 4-5).

The signs of God's kingdom are acts of compassion and justice. Healing human brokenness, overcoming human bondage, and alleviating suffering validate the presence of God's kingdom. Christ's ministry restored the beauty and perfection of creation, and we engage in his ministry whenever we perform the works of compassion and justice that Christ performed. We extend his ministry. We are his presence in the world.

Let me hasten to say that I do not believe that the living, reigning Christ is limited or restricted by our actions. He is the sovereign Lord of the universe, has all authority both in heaven and on earth, and reigns at the right hand of God. He can and does work in mysterious and mighty ways to restore his broken creation.

The person who received the 2006 Nobel Peace Prize probably has done more to alleviate poverty in Bangladesh than anyone else. He is a Muslim. Christ works through people who do not believe in him and people of all religions. Indeed he works through his adversaries and enemies. He surely works through governments, organizations, industries, and businesses.

But those who believe in Christ become his representatives, extending Christ's ministry of reconciliation, restoration, and re-creation. We become Christ's body in the world, the temple of his Spirit, his living presence continuing to perform his works. These are works of mercy and kindness, works of healing and help, works of peace and pardon.

These works can be as simple as taking a meal to a homebound friend or as complex as negotiating peace between warring nations. These works can be as spontaneous as offering aid to a homeless person or as organized as a community development project. They can be performed by the youngest of children to the most mature adult. They can be done alone or in cooperation with others. They can be done close to home or in places far from home.

Whenever and wherever these works occur, they are to be performed in the spirit of Christ and with the mind of Christ. This is to say that these acts are offered with an attitude of humility. Jesus said, "Whenever you give alms, do not sound a trumpet before you as the hypocrites do in the synagogues and in the streets, so that they may be praised by others. Truly I tell you, they have received their reward. But when you give alms, do not let your left hand know what your right hand is doing" (Matt. 6:2-3).

On another occasion Jesus told the parable of a man praying with pride and self-satisfaction in his good life and good works. Another man who prayed refused to exalt himself and compare himself to others. The lesson of the parable is obvious: our works are not to be done to earn favor with others or with God. They do not make us better than someone else; rather, they are to be done because it is the right thing to do and because this is the kingdom and the will of God.

For this ministry of deeds, some become social workers and community organizers. Others become doctors, nurses, and health-care professionals. Still others use their personal gifts and professional training as agriculturalists, engineers, and psychologists to perform acts of compassion and justice. All of us can advocate for the powerless and work for reconciliation of all people. We can give our time, energy, and resources to care for people who are suffering.

Prophetic Ministry

The ministry of Christ, both before and after the resurrection, addresses the fundamental problem in the world—human sinfulness. Identified by some as brokenness or fallenness or darkness, the reality is that as human beings we disobey God's law, disregard God's love, and act harmfully toward others as well as toward ourselves. Sin, manifested in multiple actions and attitudes, is common to every race, every culture, every generation, and every person. Sin governs our behavior to varying degrees, but this malady, this sickness, this disorder, this fact is an undeniable problem for all humanity.

And for this problem, Christ came. He said on one occasion, "Indeed, God did not send the Son into the world to condemn the world, but in order that the world might be saved through him" (John 3:17). Yet, in fact, his life does stand as a judgment or a contradiction to human sinfulness. The purity of his motives and the beauty of his character contrast starkly with the rest of us. His righteous life, unflinching obedience to his Father's will, and awe-inspiring holiness provide a model and an example to all. So perfectly did he adhere to the will of God that he can speak sternly to hypocrisy and pretense. And he did so quite often.

Then Jesus said to the crowds and to his disciples, "The scribes and the Pharisees sit on Moses' seat; therefore, do whatever they teach you and follow it; but do not do as they do, for they do not practice what they teach."—Matthew 23: 1-3

"Woe to you, scribes and Pharisees, hypocrites! For you lock people out of the kingdom of heaven. For you do not go in yourselves, and when others are going in, you stop them."—Matthew 23:13

"Woe to you, scribes and Pharisees, hypocrites! For you tithe mint, dill, and cummin, and have neglected the weightier matters of the law: justice and mercy and faith. It is these you ought to have practiced without neglecting the others."
—Matthew 23:23

"Woe to you, scribes and Pharisees, hypocrites! For you are like whitewashed tombs, which on the outside look beautiful, but inside they are full of the bones of the dead and of all kinds of filth."
—Matthew 23:27

"Woe to you, scribes and Pharisees, hypocrites! For you build the tombs of the prophets and decorate the graves of the righteous."—Matthew 23:29

Anyone who reads the New Testament will recognize Jesus as a strong prophetic figure. In the tradition of the Hebrew prophets before him, he issues blistering rebukes to the religious leaders and establishment of his day. He confronts those whose sin enslaves others and whose participation in corrupt systems causes harm. On occasion he predicts destruction and death and promises an ultimate reckoning and accountability for every person.

If we are to continue Christ's presence in the world, we too must engage in prophetic ministry. Exactly what form this will take varies from culture to culture and will be determined by the context and times in which we are called to live. But certainly a prophetic stance will demand from each of us a life of personal holiness, a spirit of benevolence, and moral conduct above reproach. Listen to this admonition from Romans 12:9-21:

> Let love be genuine; hate what is evil, hold fast to what is good; love one another with mutual affection; outdo one another in showing honor. Do not lag in zeal, be ardent in spirit, serve the Lord. Rejoice in hope, be patient in suffering, persevere in prayer. Contribute to the needs of the saints; extend hospitality to strangers. Bless those who persecute you; bless and do not curse them. Rejoice with those who rejoice, weep with those who weep. Live in harmony with one another; do not be haughty, but associate with the lowly; do not claim to be wiser than you are. Do not repay anyone evil for evil, but take thought for what is noble in the sight of all. If it is possible, so far as it depends on you, live peaceably with all. Beloved, never avenge yourselves, but leave room for the wrath of God; for it is written, "Vengeance is mine, I will repay, says the Lord." No, "if your enemies are hungry, feed them; if they are thirsty, give them something to drink; for by doing this you will heap burning coals on their heads." Do not be overcome by evil, but overcome evil with good.

Here is another admonition from Hebrews:

> Pursue peace with everyone, and the holiness without which no one will see the Lord. See to it that no one fails to obtain the grace of God; that no root of bitterness springs up and causes trouble, and through it many become defiled.—Hebrews 12:14-15

> Let mutual love continue. Do not neglect to show hospitality to strangers, for by doing that some have entertained angels without knowing it. Remember those who are in prison, as though you were in prison with them; those who are being tortured, as though you yourselves were being tortured. Let marriage be held in honor by all, and let the marriage bed be kept undefiled; for God will judge fornicators and adulterers. Keep your lives free from the love of money, and be content with what you have; for he has said, "I will never leave you or forsake you.
> —Hebrews 13:1-5

Another admonition:

> Beloved, I urge you as aliens and exiles to abstain from the desires of the flesh that wage war against the soul. Conduct yourselves honorably among the Gentiles, so that, though they malign you as evildoers, they may see your honorable deeds and glorify God when he comes to judge.—1 Peter 2:11-12

> Since therefore Christ suffered in the flesh, arm yourselves also with the same intention (for whoever has suffered in the flesh has finished with sin), so as to live for the rest of your earthly life no longer by human desires but by the will of God. You have already spent enough time in doing what the Gentiles like to do, living in licentiousness, passions, drunkenness, revels, carousing, and lawless idolatry. They are surprised that you no longer join them in the same excesses of dissipation, and so they blaspheme. But they will have to give an accounting to him who stands ready to judge the living and the dead.—1 Peter 4:1-5

These exhortations and many others make clear that prophetic ministry begins with prophetic quality of character in those who follow Christ. The validity of our prophetic words and deeds will be determined first by the Christlike character of our own words and deeds. If we are not authentic to Christ's example in our lives, little we say or do will have an impact on the world.

If we are not honest, we cannot call for honesty in the marketplace. If we are sexually immoral and promiscuous, how can we call for fidelity in marriage or celibacy in singleness? If we are greedy and discontent, how can we rebuke a materialistic culture? If we are angry and violent, we are ill-prepared to speak or act against the pervasive violence in our world and promote peace. If we do not live simply and act generously, we will be poor prophets calling for that generosity in the wider culture. Prophetic ministry requires us first to repent of our own sin and then to repent again and again.

Only then can we call and work for repentance and change in our families, our society, and in our governments. The prophetic witness is integral to the ministry of Christ, and it is one we must not shun. Let us not be afraid or be too comfortable with our culture. Let us pray for wisdom and courage that we not be captive to the corporate sins that need prophetic witness. And then let us become involved personally and practically in ways that result in real change in the way people live.

A Priestly Ministry

Although Jesus was surely a prophet, he was far more than a prophet. No prophet before or since would claim for himself what Jesus claimed. He invites a weary and burdened humanity to come to him and then promises to give rest (see Matt. 11:28). He often predicted his death (see Matt. 16:21) and spoke of his life and death as a sacrifice to be offered as atonement for sin (see Matt. 20:28). On the night before his death, Jesus instituted a memorial meal and spoke of his body being broken and his blood being shed for the forgiveness of sins (see Matt. 26:26-28). And after his death and resurrection, he explained how these events had been predicted in the Hebrew scriptures and were necessary as a part of God's eternal plan of salvation (see Luke 24:25-27).

Jesus is Savior. His exemplary life, obedience to God, and particularly his suffering qualify him as the Great High Priest, not unlike the high priest in the Hebrew sacrificial system. However, Christ makes atonement for our sins not annually but once for all, and he does so not with the sacrifice of an animal but with the sacrifice of his own life. The unknown writer of Hebrews states it as clearly as it can be stated:

> But when Christ came as a high priest of the good things that have come, then through the greater and perfect tent (not made with hands, that is, not of this creation), he entered once for all into the Holy Place, not with the blood of goats and calves, but with his own blood, thus obtaining eternal redemption.—Hebrews 9:11-12

The priestly ministry of Jesus means that by virtue of his sacrificial death on the cross and his triumphant resurrection from the grave, he offers us forgiveness from our sins, deliverance from our sins, and triumph over our sins. He is not only prophet, rebuking our sinfulness and calling us to holiness and justice, but he is the Redeemer, the reconciler who saves us from our sins and empowers us to live our lives in holiness and justice. He not only points the way to truth and righteousness and goodness, he himself makes a way for us to experience all this.

The one word that best describes the priestly ministry of Christ is the word *grace*. John says it this way: "From his fullness we have all received, grace upon grace. The law indeed was given through Moses; grace and truth came through Jesus Christ" (John 1:16-17). The greatest of all the Hebrew prophets was Moses, the lawgiver. Jesus is much more than this great prophet. Jesus is the revelation and embodiment of God's grace. His sacrificial death is his free gift to us to make atonement for our sins. His living and loving presence is offered to us now as a free gift, and with that presence comes the offer of pardon for our past sins and freedom from our present sins. This is the priestly ministry of Jesus Christ.

How do we participate in this priestly ministry? How do we extend to others God's grace revealed in Jesus Christ? How do we help the world understand and receive the good news and taste the salvation that liberates from guilt and fear? The answer to this question, of course, begins with our own experience of grace. We cannot minister what we ourselves do not receive. If we are still living by a performance-based religion or trying to prove our worthiness or goodness before God, we show that we know little of grace.

But if by looking at the Cross we can see the image of a God who loves us so much that he enters into our suffering and bears our sin, we know we can trust this God with our lives. We can let go of our compulsions and our need to be right or to be in control. We don't have to feel guilty all the time. We don't need to be afraid of the future or afraid of failure or afraid of dying.

"If God is for us, who is against us? He who did not withhold his own Son, but gave him up for all of us, will he not with him also give us everything else?" (Rom. 8:31-32). Jesus is the ultimate victim, yet he is the willing victim. And this makes him the ultimate victor. He is victor over everything that would destroy or debilitate us.

Nothing in the entire universe can separate us from the love of God. Jesus tasted everything that sin can do to an innocent person. He was betrayed, suffered humiliation, physical pain, and isolation from God. Yet he never stopped loving. Even in the darkest hour of his life, he forgave his executioners. He offered assurances of pardon to a dying criminal at his side. He showed care for his mother and closest friend in the hour of his greatest agony. And at the moment of his death, he surrendered himself to the God he calls Father.

This is not just the death of a martyr or hero. This is the death of a Savior. So we gaze upon this cross. We meditate on Christ's suffering. We study and struggle to explain its meaning more fully. We contemplate it as an event of cosmic proportions and a mystery that redeems humanity and redeems us. The more we do this, the more we lose our pride and self-assertiveness. And the more we want to love as he loved, to sacrifice as he sacrificed, to be obedient to the will of God as he was obedient to the will of God.

Through such meditation and study we come to understand our part in Christ's priestly ministry. Recognizing that we have received grace, we now give grace. Understanding that we are forgiven, we now forgive. Seeing what unconditional love is, we now offer it to others. Being freed from our own guilt and fear, we can help others become free. Having experienced reconciliation, we can be instruments of reconciliation.

The church of Jesus Christ, more than any other place or people in the world, should be a place and people of grace helping others find peace with God, peace with one another, and peace within themselves. The church can be not only a safe place but a saving place. Receiving grace, giving grace, experiencing grace, dispensing grace constitutes a priestly ministry that continues the ministry of Christ. In this ministry we offer healing, reconciliation, and restoration.

To live out the priestly ministry, some people become therapists and counselors. Others become chaplains, pastoral counselors, and ministers in specialized settings. Still others become spiritual directors or spiritual guides. Each of these seeks to administer grace to people in life's stages of development and in life's crises. They care for the homeless, the grieving, the sick, the dying. All these are priestly ministries of grace just like care for widows, orphans, the persecuted, and refugees.

Priestly ministries can be both personal and institutional. Each and every believer is a priest before God and therefore can offer grace to someone else. We may not be professionally trained, but we can listen compassionately to a grieving friend. We can practice hospitality and open our homes and hearts to strangers. We can visit the sick or dying. We can also support institutions devoted to the ministry of grace among those considered forgotten or failures. Hospitals and hospices, orphanages and retirement homes, rescue missions and community centers, clinics, shelters, and relief organizations are only some of the institutional expressions of priestly ministry where we can be the presence of Christ.

Reflection Questions

1. "We will engage in ministry out of our giftedness and in collaboration with others." How have you identified your gifts and temperament? If you have not thought about it before, try describing these now. How does your ministry fit within the larger context of Christ's ministry?

2. Christ combined in himself all the aspects of ministry (word and deed, and practice of grace and healing). How can we as individuals do the same? How does this total description apply to the church as a corporate body?

3. We often hear the word *holistic* used to describe Christlikeness. Recall examples from your past when individuals or churches were distorted or one-sided in their ministry attempts. Imagine those situations being healed by Christ. How would they have been different?

CHAPTER 9

Peace and Justice

Becoming the Presence of Christ for the World

Can people with a kingdom perspective make a difference in this broken world? Can we, in spite of theological differences, find ways to work collaboratively for justice and reconciliation, for peace and prosperity? Can we put aside divisive rhetoric to address the horrendous problems facing humankind? I believe we can! And for the sake of survival, we must!

Consider some sobering facts from *Fifty Facts That Should Change the World* by Jessica Williams:

- One-third of the world's population is at war. In 2002, 30 countries were fighting in 37 armed conflicts—a combined population of 2.29 billion.

- One in five people live on less than $1.00 per day.

- HIV/AIDS infects 36 million people worldwide with 20 million in sub-Saharan Africa.

- The world's trade in illegal drugs is about the same as the world's pharmaceutical industry.

- Two billion people in the world suffer chronic malnutrition.[1]

These kinds of statistics demand attention from all people of goodwill. They literally shout at us, challenging our conscience and calling us to action. For those of us who desire to be the presence of Christ in the world, these kinds of statistics describe a reality that is simply unacceptable because it contradicts the kingdom of God.

We must become activists and advocates for social justice because we are activists and advocates for the kingdom of God on earth as it is in heaven. First, we receive this kingdom into our lives, and then we view all of life from a kingdom perspective.

Seek a Kingdom Perspective

Righteousness and justice characterize the kingdom of God, and Jesus came to announce, embody, and inaugurate the kingdom of God. The kingdom was the unifying vision in all of Jesus' preaching and teaching and the primary motif of his parables. In fact, Jesus called the reality and availability of the kingdom of God the good news.

What is the kingdom of God? It's the divine order of reality that results when and where God's sovereignty and lordship is fully realized. Jesus himself incarnated that divine order. The nature and character of his life perfectly illustrates what it looks like. If you want to know what the kingdom of God is and what are its results, simply observe the life of Jesus as he lived on this earth. The qualities of life that he admonishes in us are the qualities he exhibited fully and perfectly during his brief time here.

The kingdom Jesus incarnated and exhibited is the divine order that has come, is coming, and will come in its future fullness.

This order has already dawned within human history; we can glimpse it among us, though imperfectly, in churches, cells, and congregations. But it awaits consummation. When the kingdom comes in its fullness, there will be justice for all the oppressed. There will be no disparity between rich and poor, no divide between people because of race or social class. There will be no violence and aggression, and there will be peace.

As individuals in whom the presence of Christ dwells, we are to seek this kingdom above all else. We are to order our lives according to its ethic and pattern our behavior after the one who incarnated it. We are to serve this kingdom, pray for its coming, and live expectantly for its full realization.

At present we live in an in-between time. The kingdom has "already" come, but the kingdom has "not yet" come in its fullness. Our passion for the kingdom in the here and now will cause us to seek kingdom justice during this in-between time. It's not that we bring in the kingdom or even extend the kingdom. God does that because it is God's kingdom. But we can live, work, and pray for the realization of that kingdom in the here and now.

Can people with a kingdom perspective make a difference in this broken world? Can we, in spite of theological differences, find ways to work collaboratively for justice and reconciliation, for peace and prosperity? Can we put aside divisive rhetoric to address the horrendous problems facing humankind? I believe we can! And for the sake of survival, we must!

Simplify Your Life

In the struggle for justice, a good place to act is with our own values and lifestyle. Do they reflect allegiance to the kingdom of God or allegiance to the kingdoms of this world? Jesus depicts a stark contrast between these two perspectives:

> Do not store up for yourselves treasures on earth,
> where moth and rust consume and where thieves

break in and steal; . . . No one can serve two masters; for a slave will either hate the one and love the other, or be devoted to the one and despise the other. You cannot serve God and wealth. Therefore I tell you, do not worry about your life, what you will eat or what you will drink, or about your body, what you will wear. Is not life more than food, and the body more than clothing? . . . But strive first for the kingdom of God and his righteousness, and all these things will be given to you as well.—Matthew 6:19, 24-25, 33

Jeffrey Sachs in his book *The End of Poverty* reports the startling statistic that every year more than eight million people around the world die because they are simply too poor to survive. That translates into twenty thousand deaths daily. Sachs writes:

The poor die in hospital wards that lack drugs, in villages that lack antimalarial bed nets, in houses that lack safe drinking water. They die namelessly, without public comment. Sadly, such stories rarely get written. Most people are unaware of the daily struggles for survival, and of the vast numbers of impoverished people around the world who lose that struggle.[2]

Global poverty presents not only social, economic, and political problems but also a moral issue. How can we continue to enjoy luxury when so many are perishing? How can we justify our standard and style of life when multitudes struggle with survival? How can people of faith say they love God and not respond to the world's suffering? The global imperative of our time is justice. Can we find the moral vision, the urgent passion, the political will, and the collaborative spirit to bring an end to global poverty?

Can we afford to live in isolation and indifference amid such suffering and injustice? I don't think so! In the book *Believing in the Future*, David Bosch contends that North American culture has "an insatiable desire for self-gratification."

> People want to enjoy their football matches, rock festivals, television programs, holidays, and parties—all of which they "deserve" after a hard day's work. Sacrifice, asceticism, modesty, self-discipline, and the like, are not popular virtues.[3]

I recently visited Nairobi. While sitting around a table with several adolescent boys, I asked them, "What is the best thing in your life?" They each answered quickly with similar responses, "Jesus" or "my relationship with God," or "being a Christian."

Then I asked them, "What is the hardest thing in your life?" I was overwhelmed by their answers. The first one said, "My next meal." The next one said, "What I will eat." The next one said, "Where I will sleep tonight." Later, reflecting on this conversation, I realized how different the answers would be if I were asking those questions of adolescents (or adults) in the United States. Justice begins with our learning to live simply so that others can simply live.

Find and Use Your Voice

In this beautiful world a cosmic struggle continuously unfolds between good and evil, sin and righteousness, oppression and freedom. The outcome of that struggle has already been determined, but the ongoing struggle is very real. God is amid the struggle, and the incarnation of God in the person of Jesus is the supreme evidence of that fact. During his life and ministry Jesus participated and involved himself in this struggle in a number of ways.

Jesus encountered the devil and resisted temptation. On numerous occasions he cast evil spirits out of people. He rebuked the devil and his demons, always asserting his authority over them. It is clear from the Gospels that in such interactions, Jesus saw the struggle between good and evil as involving the unseen spirit world as well as the world of humans. Yet the struggle clearly created confrontation with humans. Jesus spoke harsh words to the religious leaders of his day. He rebuked their hypocrisy and vanity. He condemned the way they treated people and set themselves above the very ones who needed the love and grace of God.

Fearless in his words and actions, Jesus spoke directly to the demonic spirits and to the demonic spirit of certain religious authorities. He courageously addressed the leaders of a religious system that gave priority to tradition over human beings. We need this kind of courage if we are to join the struggle for social justice.

We too must speak to the evil in our midst and name it for what it is. I'm not calling for exorcisms, but I am calling for voices of conscience in the presence of real evil. Each of us in our circle of influence can speak up and speak out against dishonesty, greed, and violence. And each of us can speak for fairness, purity, and equal opportunity for all. This may sound simple, but it can be very difficult, especially when the time to speak comes in the presence of people we know.

Addressing "the principalities and powers" that enslave people and prevent them from realizing their human potential is not easy. It does take courage. Indeed, to "find your voice" and use it may be one of life's biggest challenges. Yet it is crucial in the struggle for justice. One problem I recognize in myself and in other Christians is how easy it is to be silent, to say nothing, in the face of evil.

I grew up in a culture of prejudice against African Americans. I remember hearing pastors, deacons, and good church people tell racist jokes or speak untruths about African-American people. And no one, including myself, would confront or contradict such rhetoric as sinful. I can't count how many similar conversations I've heard that demean women, and no one countered such conversation. There was a deafening silence.

It may not be that our voice will be heard on national TV or in large audiences, but that's not the point. If we speak to the demonic lies that we hear or see, it will make a difference. In our families, in our workplaces, or in our churches, we can join in the struggle for justice. We may think that our voices are not heard, but that is not our primary responsibility. It is simply to speak.

Become Political

Ultimately, if we are to enter the struggle for justice, we will engage in shaping public policy and in political activity. We will not live in the confines of our homes and churches, neglecting the complex issues that impact our neighbors. We will care about education for children, protection for the environment, and opportunities for the poor. We will not be satisfied to live in isolation from others but will act according to our circumstances and abilities to build bridges of understanding and work for everyone's welfare.

When it comes to politics and moral issues, no political party has a corner on the truth. Christians ought to be concerned about social justice, but let us be careful in choosing the issues that fit only in our political persuasion. The United States faces a crisis of sexual immorality and promiscuity. We have reason to be concerned about the erosion of the family and the attacks on the sanctity of marriage as well as the loss of respect for the unborn. We ought also to be concerned about the growing disparity between rich and poor and the fact that forty million Americans don't have health insurance.

We are witnessing an unprecedented abuse of the environment as well as a pervasive indifference to violence and pornography in this country. Racism remains a cancer that eats at the very fabric of our society. There are an array of global issues that Christians need to face: proliferation of nuclear weapons, terrorism, nation building in the developing world, and the pandemic of HIV/AIDS. Quality education for all Americans as well as affordable and quality health care for all Americans are moral issues. I could go on and on.

Being the presence of Christ involves political awareness, concern, and action in the world. With all this in mind, let me make several suggestions.

Be a participant and protagonist in the political process. Vote your conscience and vote for the candidates of your choice, then hold those candidates accountable. Write letters to your elected officials and to the newspapers. Use your voice to make known your convictions. Enter into the political debate and political process.

Don't be so partisan that you can't envision compromise and collaboration with those of different perspectives to achieve common goals. Some people are so partisan in their politics that they have difficulty relating honestly and warmly to others who do not share their views. This is unfortunate, but among Christians, it is inexcusable. Why? Because we owe ultimate allegiance not to our own country (no matter how much we love it) and not to any political party (no matter how much we are committed). Because we are disciples of Christ, our ultimate devotion is to the kingdom of God that transcends all political boundaries, systems, and parties.

In addition to an ultimate commitment to the kingdom of God, we can *cultivate a global perspective.* Our nation is one of hundreds. Scripture clear states that God is Lord over all nations and governments. Scripture also clearly affirms that God loves all people, regardless of the nation or country in which they live. All of God's children are precious, and we cannot claim any privileged place because we are Americans. A global perspective will cause us to act, pray, and think differently than if we act, think, and pray only in nationalistic ways.

Work for bipartisanship in addressing domestic as well as global concerns of our day. Debate is necessary in a democracy. Differences are inevitable, but we need politicians who act more like statesmen and stateswomen than opportunists and ideologues. Encourage our leaders to reach compromise, practice collaboration, and find ways to work together to resolve real problems.

Consider the following prayer we can offer for ourselves and others who enter into the struggle for justice in the public and political process. It was crafted by American theologian Reinhold Niebuhr but may have older origins. Certainly Niebuhr understood both the value and limits of politics.

God, grant me the serenity to accept the things I
   cannot change;
the courage to change the things I can,
and the wisdom to know the difference.

First, we should *pray for serenity*. No matter how much I fret about them, I cannot change many policies of the government. Some realities and circumstances exist beyond my power to control. However, serenity is not the same as indifference. It is not passive resignation or just another word for denial. Serenity is born out of quiet confidence that there is a providence greater than our accountability. Serenity "surpasses all understanding" and defies logic.

Pray for courage. There are at least two kinds of courage: the heroic act of self-sacrifice in a time of crisis and sustained and principled action for change. Eugene Peterson calls the latter "a long obedience in the same direction."[4] Courage of this kind is equally heroic as the first type because often it is exhibited in the face of opposition and without apparent results.

Pray for wisdom. The great challenge is, of course, knowing which things to accept and which things to change. Knowing when to speak up and when to be silent. Knowing when to act and when to wait. When it comes to politics, there is neither a rule book nor a perfect politician. So we need wisdom.

Perhaps we find a clue to the kind of wisdom we need in the book of James: "the wisdom from above is first pure, then peaceable, gentle, willing to yield, full of mercy and good fruits without a trace of partiality or hypocrisy" (Jas. 3:17). This kind of wisdom does not discount political passion but controls it, checks it, and even channels it. Wisdom not only offers discernment on how to know the difference between what can and cannot be changed, but it creates a different context in which we express our political passions.

Do not be afraid! To be an advocate and activist for justice, one cannot be fainthearted. It requires courage and perseverance, especially in a polarized culture. We are living in tumultuous and tense times. Perhaps it has always been so, but I feel keenly the stress and strain of the world that is ever present and ever pressing upon us. In reaction to these tense times a rising tide of fear and fundamentalism offers slick slogans, simplistic answers, and quick fixes to long-standing, complex problems.

We seem caught between two horns of a cultural dilemma. On the one hand is a secularist, materialistic, and hedonistic society, while on the other are highly offended religionists who would seek to impose narrow and strict interpretations of faith on everyone. Perhaps no one else feels this tension, but I do.

I deplore the loss of respect for human life, the decline of private and public morality, the diminishing of personal responsibility and the general permissiveness in our society. At the same time, however, I am not comfortable with a perspective that equates Christian faith with only one political perspective, seems blind to racial and economic justice, and allows little room for dissent and disagreement.

Perhaps many of us are seeking a "third way," "a different way," "a new way," maybe even "a radical way." We desire to hold our Christian faith close to our hearts, but we also desire to have genuine friendship and dialogue with people of other faiths to build human community. We do believe that the story and truth of scripture comes from God, but we want to preserve the freedom of conscience that allows for different interpretations.

We want to be the presence of Christ with conviction but also with compassion. We desire to be a part of the world's transformation, but we are painfully aware that we ourselves need to be transformed. We feel the need to be humble and gentle with those who may view life differently from us, but we also desire to be unashamed of what we have experienced as good news in Jesus Christ.

In the struggle for justice we need the reminder of the words Jesus spoke to the women immediately after the Resurrection: "Do not be afraid." The living Christ who is within us is also before us. His presence and providence are at work in this broken world in ways that are often hidden to us. His kingdom that has come has yet to come in all of its fullness. Indeed the day will dawn when "the earth will be full of the knowledge of the LORD as the waters cover the sea" (Isa. 11:9).

We need not be afraid.

Reflection Questions

1. "We become activists and advocates for social justice because we are activists and advocates for the kingdom of God on earth as it is in heaven." If this is so, how is the kingdom of God different from the world order in which we live?

2. Whom do you most admire as Christian advocates and activists for social justice?

3. What is the difference between being politically involved as a Christian and identifying the gospel of Jesus Christ with your political perspective?

AFTERWORD

This brief book, a primer on the Christian gospel, makes the audacious claim that global transformation can take place as the risen Christ lives in and through those who follow him. I have set forth the "presence of Christ" as a reality that we can receive, nurture, practice, experience, and express.

In conclusion, on the following pages I share four poetic offerings for personal or communal devotions:

> a confession of faith
> a doxology
> a witness
> a prayer

These summarize the reality in which I live my own life and which I desire for others.

A Confession of Faith

I worship the living, loving God, Creator and Sustainer
of all that exists.
I follow Jesus as the Messiah of Israel, the image and incarnation
of the invisible God, the Savior for all humanity
and the crucified, resurrected Lord.
I trust the Spirit, present and active in the world,
in the church and in the lives of individuals.
I read the scriptures, Old and New Testaments,
as divinely inspired records
of God's self-revelation, the written word of God.
I love the kingdom of God—God's order of things —
as present in Jesus
and now available to all who accept it.
I celebrate the mystical presence of Christ in the gathered church
and the continued mission of Christ in the scattered church.
I anticipate life beyond death, the resurrection of the body, a final
judgment and a future glory that words cannot describe.

I cherish
the truth and beauty of prayer,
the sanctity and goodness of life,
the redemptive power of pain and suffering,
the pure joy of family and friends.

I affirm the freedom of conscience and competency
of all persons
to respond to God for themselves.
I believe in the love and grace of God for all people,
including those whose confession is different than this one.

A Doxology

You have come. Blessed and holy be your name
Babe in the manger
Only begotten of the Father. Wisdom and word of God
Visible image of the invisible
Life, light, love

You come. Blessed and holy be your name.
Crucified and risen
Spirit of truth, Paraclete, Comforter, Advocate
Given all authority in heaven and on earth
Life, light, love

You will come. Blessed and holy be your name
Lord of lords, King of kings
Judge of humankind, Maker of a new heaven and a new earth
Lamb enthroned, worthy of worship
Life, light, love

A Witness

The Christ I follow is the crucified, resurrected Lord.
His teachings embody the truth of God.
His deeds, called miracles or signs, are evidences of God's
kingdom—a divine order of reality.
His life is an image of the glory of God.
His death is a revelation of the love of God.
His resurrection is the result of the power of God.

This wounded, ever-living One empowers us to accept forgiveness
for our sins and freedom from our fears. Christ promises an
abiding companionship, invites us to engage in God's continuing
mission of redemption and share in the world's suffering.

Participation in Christ means participation in a community.
Some in the community have already passed the divide between
time and eternity. They cheer us on in our struggles and wait
for us to join them. All in this global community share
a mystical bond and a common hope.

Human misery and unexplained evil create unanswered
questions and unresolved mystery. But in Christ I have
discovered faith, hope and love.

Because of Christ . . .

the universe is sensible;
death is acceptable;
the world is beautiful;
sorrow is bearable;
life is meaningful.

A Prayer

You are the wounded Messiah whom God raised from the dead.
And now by your Spirit you live among and within all who
believe in you.
We are
Your Holy Temple
Your Mystical Body
Your Continuing Presence.

Since no individual and no group of individuals
can exhaust your meaning,
All are necessary.
The richness of your character and ministry finds expression
in the richness of your Church.
Some of us convey your gentle compassion and
tender mercies better than others.
Some of us reflect your stern rebukes and passion for
justice better than others.
Some of us are ecstatic,
Some of us are contemplative.
You live in each. Each lives in you.

Grant, O crucified Living One,
That our union and communion be completed.
Our life and love be perfected,
Our spirits, inhabited by your Spirit,
Redound to the glory of God and the redemption of all creation.

NOTES

CHAPTER 1

1. Harry D. Clarke, "Into My Heart," at http://www.cyberhymnal.org/htm/i/m/y/inmyheart.htm

CHAPTER 3

1. This phrase comes from a seventeenth-century book *The Practice of the Presence of God*, written by Nicholas Herman, aka Brother Lawrence.

2. Parker J. Palmer, in his book *Let Your Life Speak: Listening for the Voice of Vocation* (San Francisco: Jossey-Bass, 2000), has a chapter titled "There Is a Season," describing life's stages as seasons.

3. C. S. Lewis, *The World's Last Night* (New York: Harcourt, Brace and World, 1960), 4.

4. For further reading and explanation about keeping Sabbath, see Tilden Edwards, *Sabbath Time,* rev. ed. (Nashville, TN: Upper Room Books, 2003).

5. Johnson Oatman Jr., "Count Your Blessings," in *The Baptist Hymnal* (Nashville, TN: Convention Press, 1991), no. 644.

6. *The Spiritual Exercises of St. Ignatius*, trans. Anthony Mottola (New York: Image Books, 1964).

CHAPTER 4

1. Paul Julius Alexander, *The Patriarch Nicephorus of Constantinople: Ecclesiastical Policy and Image Worship in the Byzantine Empire* (Oxford: Clarendon Press, 1958), 5, quoted in Jaroslav J. Pelikan, *The Spirit of Eastern Christendom* (Chicago: University of Chicago Press, 1977), 93.

2. Reginald Heber, "Holy, Holy, Holy! Lord God Almighty," in *The United Methodist Hymnal* (Nashville, TN: United Methodist Publishing House, 1989), no. 77.

3. For further explanation of the Jesus Prayer, see *The Art of Prayer: An Orthodox Anthology*, comp. Igumen Chariton of Valamo, trans. E. Kadlovbosky and E. M. Palmer (London: Faber and Faber Limited, 1966).

4. For further explanation on Centering Prayer, see Thomas Keating, *Open Mind, Open Heart: The Contemplative Dimension of the Gospel* (New York: Continuum, 1994) or M. Basil Pennington, *Centering Prayer: Renewing an Ancient Christian Prayer Form* (Garden City, NY: Image Books, 1982).

CHAPTER 5

1. Thomas Merton, *Contemplation in a World of Action* (Garden City, NY: Image Books, 1973), 175–76.

2. Ibid., 176–77.

3. Dietrich Bonhoeffer, *Life Together* (New York: Harper & Row Publishers, 1954), 29.

4. Thomas O. Chisholm, "Great Is Thy Faithfulness," in *United Methodist Hymnal*, no. 140.

5. Palmer, *Let Your Life Speak*, 73.

CHAPTER 6

1. Jaroslav Pelikan, *Jesus Through the Centuries: His Place in the History of Culture* (New Haven, CT: Yale University Press, 1985), table of contents.

2. Vincent J. Donovan, *Christianity Rediscovered: An Epistle from the Masai* (London: SCM Press, 1982), 200.

CHAPTER 9

1. Jessica Williams, *Fifty Facts That Should Change the World* (New York: The Disinformation Co., 2004).

2. Jeffrey D. Sachs, *The End of Poverty: Economic Possibilities for Our Time* (New York: Penguin Press: New York, 2005), 1.

3. David J. Bosch, *Believing in the Future* (Harrisburg, PA: Trinity Press International, 1995), 3.

4. Eugene H. Peterson, *A Long Obedience in the Same Direction: Discipleship in an Instant Society*, 20th Anniversary Edition (Downers Grove, IL: InterVarsity Press, 2000).

ABOUT THE AUTHOR

DANIEL VESTAL has been a voice for Christian discipleship for over forty years. He is a leader within the Baptist denomination and has been involved in ecumenical efforts and interfaith dialogue. Since 1996 he has been executive coordinator of the Cooperative Baptist Fellowship. Daniel and his wife, Earlene, have three children and five grandchildren. They live in Atlanta, Georgia.